Description

Innovative Practices for Archives and Special Collections Series Editor: Kate Theimer

This dynamic series is aimed at those working in archives and special collections as well as other cultural heritage organizations. It also provides students and faculty in archives, library, and public history graduate programs a resource for understanding the issues driving change in the field today.

Each book in the series tackles a different area in the field of archives and special collections librarianship and demonstrates the kinds of strategies archivists are using to meet these new challenges.

These innovative practices reflect approaches and ideas that will be new to many readers. The case studies featured in each book have been selected to keep in mind a broad spectrum of readers and enable the series, as a whole, to benefit a diverse audience.

Each book features case studies from both large and small organizations. Thus, some of the creative ideas presented are being implemented with costly tools and robust infrastructures, and others are being done on a shoestring. A hallmark of the series is that every case study incorporates ideas that are transferrable, even if the specific implementation might not be.

About the Series Editor

Kate Theimer is the author of the popular blog *ArchivesNext* and a frequent writer, speaker, and commentator on issues related to the future of archives. She is the author of *Web 2.0 Tools and Strategies for Archives and Local History Collections* and the editor of *A Different Kind of Web: New Connections between Archives and Our Users*, as well as having contributed chapters to *Many Happy Returns: Advocacy for Archives and Archivists, The Future of Archives and Recordkeeping* and the forthcoming *Encyclopedia of Archival Concepts, Principles, and Practices*. She has published articles in *The American Archivist* and the *Journal of Digital Humanities*.

Kate served on the Council of the Society of American Archivists from 2010 to 2013. Before starting her career as an independent writer and editor, she worked in the policy division of the National Archives and Records Administration in College Park, Maryland.

Titles in the Series

Description: Innovative Practices for Archives and Special Collections
Outreach: Innovative Practices for Archives and Special Collections
Reference and Access: Innovative Practices for Archives and Special Collections
Management: Innovative Practices for Archives and Special Collections

Description

Innovative Practices for Archives and Special Collections

Edited by Kate Theimer

ROWMAN & LITTLEFIELD
Lanham • Boulder • New York • Toronto • Plymouth, UK

Published by Rowman & Littlefield
4501 Forbes Boulevard, Suite 200, Lanham, Maryland 20706
www.rowman.com

10 Thornbury Road, Plymouth PL6 7PP, United Kingdom

British Library Cataloguing in Publication Information Available

Library of Congress Cataloging-in-Publication Data

Description / edited by Kate Theimer.
pages cm. -- (Innovative practices for archives and special collections ; 1) Includes bibliographical references and index.
Includes bibliographical references and index.
ISBN 978-0-8108-9093-0 (pbk.) -- ISBN 978-0-8108-9094-7 (ebook) 1. Cataloging of archival materials. 2. Cataloging of archival materials--Case studies. 3. Cataloging of special collections in libraries. 4. Cataloging of special collections in libraries--Case studies. 5. Information storage and retrieval systems--Archival materials. I. Theimer, Kate, 1966- editor of compilation.
Z695.2.D47 2014
025.3'414--dc23
2013048845

Printed in the United States of America

Contents

Introduction

Most archivists would agree that the reason we collect and preserve the materials in our collections is so that they can be accessed and used. However, for the majority of researchers, it is the descriptions of collections that must first be successfully accessed and understood in order to locate the right materials. Effective access depends on good description. However, what constitutes "good" description—or, perhaps, "good enough" description—is a topic of constant and necessary discussion in the profession. An essential part of that discussion is how best to tackle creating those descriptions. How should limited resources be used or supplemented? What strategies or approaches should be employed? What kinds of descriptions make the most sense to the most people looking for the kinds of materials we have? At what level—collection, series, folder, or item—should materials be described? Technology plays a key role in both facilitating description and in making it accessible. What tools make sense for different kinds of archives and how can they be used? The answers to those questions are as diverse as the range of repositories responsible for historical collections.

Description: Innovative Practices for Archives and Special Collections explores how archives of different sizes and types have approached these questions, all with the common goal of increasing the accessibility of their holdings. These case studies show a range of concerns and strategies, but all were selected because they demonstrate ideas that could be transferred into many other settings. They can serve as models, sources of inspiration, or starting points for new discussions. This volume is useful to those working in archives and special collections as well as other cultural heritage organizations and provides ideas ranging from those that require long-term planning and coordination to ones that can be immediately implemented. It also provides students and educators in archives, library, and public history graduate programs a resource for understanding the varieties of ways materials are being described in the field today and the kinds of strategies archivists are using to ensure collections can be found by the people who want to use them.

ABOUT THE INNOVATIVE PRACTICES SERIES

I debated with myself for some time over the title of this series, *Innovative Practices for Archives and Special Collections*. After all, what is innovative and new to one person is often standard procedure to another. Another option was to call them "best practices" and follow the model of a series of similar books from the same publisher featuring case studies from libraries. But "best practices" seemed equally problematic. In a field that seems to embrace the phrase "it depends" as a mantra, putting forward the experience of any one archive as best practice seemed ill advised.

It is the very diversity of our field, though, that caused me to stick with my "innovative" label rather than shying away from it. There are new ideas in these books, or at least ideas that will be new to many readers. My philosophy in selecting case studies for the books in this series has been to keep in mind a broad spectrum of readers and to position the series so that it will be as valuable as possible for a diverse audience. In each book you will find case studies from both big organizations and small ones. Some of the creative ideas are being implemented with costly tools and robust infrastructures, and others are being done on a shoestring. In determining what to include, I wanted to ensure that every case study incorporates ideas that are transferrable, even if the specific implementation might not be.

This commitment to making the series broadly valuable and practical has meant striving for a balance that favors more approachable innovations over implementations that are aggressively on the cutting edge. The ideas presented here are within the reach of most archives and special collections—if not right away, then in the near future. They represent the creativity and commitment to serving and expanding our audiences that I think are the defining characteristics of the archival profession in the early 21st century.

Because archival functions and processes are interrelated and don't always fit neatly into compartments, and because most archivists perform several of them in the course of their daily work, the contents of each of the volumes in this series has both its own clear focus and overlapping relationships with the others. Case studies in reference and access touch inevitably on description and outreach. Since the overarching purpose of description is to facilitate use, issues relating to reference, access, and outreach are components of the case studies in that volume. The overlap of the management volume with all of the others should not be surprising, though the focus of the case studies there are more explicitly on management issues. These interrelationships are inevitable given the nature of archival work, and most practitioners and students will find all of the volumes useful.

Just as the activities archivists undertake depend on each other, so have I depended on the assistance of my friends and colleagues who generously agreed to review the case studies. My thanks to Rodney Carter, Amy Cooper Cary, Mary Manning, and Tanya Zanish-Belcher for the time and careful consideration they have given to improving the books in this series.

ABOUT THE DESCRIPTION CASE STUDIES

Deconstructing description into its essential elements, and including case studies that addressed all of these elements, provides an overarching rationale for the selection of contributions to this volume. In a broad sense, the description function can be broken down by considering:

- What is being described?
- Who is doing the work?
- How is the work being done?
- How are the descriptions made available?

The authors of the case studies in this collection answer those questions in a variety of ways, but each has found solutions that worked for his or her own needs. Although the use of standards enters into most of their discussions, standards by themselves don't dictate uniformity of solutions. All the authors have approached their problems by considering what will work best in their own environments and for their users. Internal needs for better description often play a role as well; increased intellectual control can be used to more effectively manage and provide reference services for collections. But perhaps the common thread running through all of these examples of innovative practices is a commitment to increasing the discoverability of archival collections. In what ways, then, do the case studies in this collection demonstrate innovation in these aspects of description?

Several case studies show different approaches to the question of what should be described. The article contributed by Erin Faulder, Veronica Martzahl, and Eliot Wilczek about their experience implementing Encoded Archival Context (EAC) at Tufts University, as well as Clare Paterson's case study about the Empowering the User project at the University of Glasgow, both reflect the recent trend in archival description to describe the creators and contributors to collections, as well as the materials themselves. Both projects also explored, with similar conclusions, the viability of describing functions separately from the materials that resulted from them.

Given its prominence in the professional discourse, solutions to the problem of efficiently describing materials in processing backlogs are necessary to include. Matthew B. Gorham and Chela Scott Weber describe their experiences conducting a comprehensive collections survey at the Brooklyn Historical Society. Eira Tansey shares a solution to a problem of a different kind: her multistage approach to migrating a backlog of finding aids into formats for 21st-century access, as well as for strategically approaching the backlog of undescribed collections at Tulane University's Louisiana Research Collection.

The description of single items has not traditionally been a priority in most archival repositories, but James Gerencser relates how access to easy-to-use technology inspired the Dickinson College Archives and Special Collections to tackle describing a long-standing legacy of single items with the goal of attracting new users. Similarly, a collection of ephemera at the University of Alberta with both a long history and an active acquisition policy inspires a pragmatic approach to item-level cataloging. Technology serves as both a platform and a driver for Kelcy Shepherd and Kate Gerrity's case study on establishing workflows for description of digitized materials at Amherst College and for Jackie Dean and Meg Tuomala's report on their progress describing born-digital collections at the University of North Carolina at Chapel Hill.

Although professionally trained archivists and special collections librarians are primarily responsible for the final products of descriptive processes, using a variety of people to contribute to or create descriptive information is another way archives are exploring new ways to approach description. Crowdsourcing is a strategy much on the minds of many archivists, and Zoë D'Arcy discusses the success of "the Hive" at the National Archives of Australia in harnessing volunteer labor online to help make creator-supplied inventory lists accessible and searchable. Evyn Kropf needed to find a way to engage a very different kind of "crowd" to assist in the cataloging of Islamic manuscripts at the University of Michigan, and her case study discusses both their successful and less-successful attempts to do so.

Kristjana Kristinsdóttir relates a radical approach to the problems of scale and limited resources by the National Archives of Iceland: making records creators responsible for the arrangement and description of their records, to archival standards, prior to their accession into the archives. Through a gradual exploration of policies and approaches, as well as patient work, Kristinsdóttir has a successful model that may work in other settings.

Good communication and training were key to the eventual success at the National Archives of Iceland, and Tansey brings up those factors again as key to success in working with the vendors who supported parts of the finding aid migration project at Tulane. An important aspect of Shepherd and Gerrity's case study about the description of digitized materials is the use of library cataloging staff to create item-level metadata and the adjustments that were necessary when making that shift. Employing graduate students to assist in archival processing is a common practice, but the case studies from Kropf and Tansey, as well as Farnel, Cole, Desmarais, Holizki, and Papineau at the University of Alberta, all discuss how descriptive projects were specifically designed to best take advantage of the skills the students had to offer. Gerencser goes further, outlining a project that was not only designed to be staffed primarily by undergraduate students but also for which undergraduate learning is seen as a key outcome.

The question of how the description work described in the case studies was carried out has answers as individual as the approaches they describe, and in many ways those approaches were shaped by the resources available. Some, like the work at the Brooklyn Historical Society and the University of Michigan, were funded by grants and involved the hiring of project staff. Grant funding also allowed the projects at Tufts and Glasgow University to create the technological environments they needed to create and publish EAC records. Securing additional funding at Tulane allowed Tansey to tap into an existing relationship with vendors to help support finding aid migration. In contrast, the other projects shared in the book demonstrate the creative use of existing funds and resources to explore new models for getting materials described.

Systems of some kind provide the infrastructure necessary for creating and sharing descriptions. The projects at the University of Alberta and Dickinson College take advantage of systems already in use to support description in new ways, while dedicated project sites were created for "the Hive" and Empowering the User. Open-source tools are used by some institutions—the Archivists' Toolkit at the Brooklyn Historical Society and Amherst College, and Archon at Tulane—while for others, propriety systems make more sense.

Another way to consider the work discussed in the case studies is whether they represent projects or changes to the program. The projects at Brooklyn, Michigan, Glasgow, and Tulane are just that: projects, with defined starting and ending points. On the other hand, the innovative practices displayed by Tufts, Amherst, University of Alberta, Dickinson College, University of North Carolina at Chapel Hill, and the National Archives of Iceland were integrated, or are planned to be integrated, into standard workflows. For the majority in both cases, however, the work outlined in the case studies has generated policies and practices that are being integrated into the regular descriptive workflows of the repository.

Because increased access is the goal of all these innovative descriptive practices, all the products they created are being made available online, often in more than one way. Some are using software like LibGuides (University of Alberta), Drupal (Dickinson), or WordPress (Brooklyn Historical Society), while others are using unique websites (the National Archives of Australia, University of Michigan, and the University of Glasgow). Some practices result in the creation of traditional finding aids, while others create descriptions in other formats. In most cases, descriptive information is being shared through the existing online catalog or website, often in addition to other platforms. Increasing discoverability, within resource limitations, is a factor all the authors considered, and for all of them the primary platform for discovery is the web.

Although each case study in this collection describes a specific response to a challenge or opportunity, I think each also reflects a philosophy of experimentation that is perhaps the most critical ingredient necessary for any organization interested in developing its own "innovative" practices. In this regard, I hope this book and the others in the series encourage all readers to consider how their own work could benefit from the exploration of new ideas and tools. This series of books can, by definition, include only a small sample of the kinds of approaches being developed by archives and special collections around the world to meet the challenges of staying relevant and adaptable in today's complex environment. These case studies give readers many useful ideas to consider—and quite possibly the inspiration to come up with tomorrow's innovations.

ONE

"The Hive"

Crowdsourcing the Description of Collections

Zoë D'Arcy, National Archives of Australia

In recent years, many galleries, libraries, archives, and museums (or GLAMs) have developed a wide range of crowdsourcing websites in an effort to capitalize on public interest to enhance and enrich their collections. Merriam-Webster's dictionary defines crowdsourcing as "the practice of obtaining needed services, ideas, or content by soliciting contributions from a large group of people, and especially from an online community, rather than from traditional employees or suppliers."[1] The crowdsourcing projects undertaken by GLAMs have taken many forms, from tagging and identifying the content in photos on sites like the Flickr Commons to "georectifying" maps on tools like the New York Public Library's Map Warper.[2] However, one of the most commons ways GLAMS have harnessed the contributions of the "crowd" has been to offer images of textual materials for the public to transcribe.

In late 2012, the National Archives of Australia launched a website called "the arcHive," (http://transcribe.naa.gov.au/). Also known as "the Hive," this crowdsourcing initiative sought to draw upon the willingness of people to help produce usable text for researchers, but this project's goal is also to engage the public more directly in the work of the archives. The Hive encourages members of the public to assist the National Archives in creating usable descriptions of materials in the backlog of collections that aren't listed on our online database, RecordSearch. The ultimate aim of the project is to use this crowdsourced data entry to increase the number of descriptions that are available in RecordSearch.

An online community has sprung up around the Hive and those who work daily on the site, and who are therefore improving access to the Archives' collection for other researchers. The Hive has much in common with other transcription projects, but it is unusual in that it challenges the assumption that online public engagement with archival records is limited to being at the very end of the access process. Although our path to involving the crowd in the work of our professional archivists has not always been a smooth one, our results show that this approach has significant potential for generating both the engagement with the public that other transcription projects do and also for offering a meaningful contribution to solving the problem of describing materials in collections backlogs.

PLANNING

The Hive was launched as one of the Archives' Labs Environment projects. The Labs Environment features small-scale projects that enable the Archives to explore new ideas and technologies in a low-cost, low-risk way.[3] The Hive website was conceived as a way of assisting our experiment with public transcription in a way that might also assist us in meeting a key performance target.

We envisioned the Hive as an innovative way to facilitate description of our collection at the file level.[4] The National Archives of Australia has only about 25 percent of its collection described (and therefore easily discoverable) on its collection database, RecordSearch. This equates to 10 million files or objects from a collection that comprises about 40 million files or objects. The scale of the Archives' collection is enormous. A few years ago, a staff member calculated that with current resources and using current description techniques, it would take the Archives 200 years to get its collection fully described at the file level. Despite this, we at the Archives have set ourselves a challenging target—to have the entire collection described on RecordSearch by the year 2030.

To help meet this target, we wanted to take advantage of the availability of consignment lists—listings at the file level that accompany each series of records when they are transferred to the Archives. In theory, a consignment list is supposed to exist for each series of records, so there are probably around 100,000 lists that we can draw upon to help jump-start our descriptive process. This approach represented a change in how we thought about the value of consignment lists, which traditionally have been used by Archives staff not to describe the collection but to help our most dedicated researchers find materials that weren't described on RecordSearch.

The consignment lists haven't previously been used to describe the collection because they are of varying quality. For instance, records transferred to the Archives in the 1950s only sometimes had consignment lists, and those lists tended to be handwritten with limited information about each file. Sometimes there might only be a number for each file or other information that was seemingly meaningless to most users. As record-transfer processes improved, so did the consignment lists. By the 1980s, the Archives' record depositors were required to provide typed or computer-printed consignment lists, so that they could be stringently checked for accuracy, and the title descriptions were generally of a high standard. This variability has meant that instead of using these lists for description, the process of records description has, up until now, been a time-consuming job that requires Archives staff to pull boxes off shelves and enter the descriptive data by looking at the files themselves.

However, researchers don't have the same opportunity to go through the contents of all the boxes on our shelves, and so the consignment lists have remained an important tool to give those who want to explore an unlisted series in our collection a glimpse of the records. Until recently, providing access to those consignment lists has always been a service limited to researchers in our Reading Rooms. As most of our researchers are online rather than visiting us in person, any knowledge gleaned from access to the lists was thus only made available to a small percentage of people. Recognizing this disparity, as well as how valuable the lists would be to all researchers, a proposal was made by staff who work with researchers that the lists be digitized and made available online to the public. This would also make the work of Reading Room staff to provide access to consignment lists more sustainable. Digitizing the lists was quickly recognized as an initiative that had the potential to benefit the Archives in many ways.

There was some uncertainty at first about where the scanned consignment lists could and should be posted. There was consensus that RecordSearch wasn't the place to put consignment lists, as it might be unclear to researchers that these images were listings of records rather than the records themselves. (Just over 3 percent of the materials listed in RecordSearch also have digital images of the records that can be viewed by the public.) Staff, particularly those who worked on collection description, were also well aware of the potential inaccuracies of the consignment lists and were concerned about providing this "raw" information on our official catalog. Keeping that information separate from RecordSearch seemed like a good risk control, and so the idea of a separate website for the lists was born. However, while the Hive was that website, it was designed from the start so that it could still enhance collection description work.

With the Labs Environment in place, we had an ideal structure available for creating and hosting a separate website for the consignment lists. We also determined that creating a new site for the consignment lists gave the Archives an ideal opportunity to explore the usefulness of some other new tools that had often been discussed within the organization but until that time were untried.

First, we wanted to try scanning the consignment list pages using Optical Character Recognition (OCR). RecordSearch currently only provides digital access to the content of collections in the form of scanned images. The only fields that can be searched to discover records are the limited metadata (such as the file and series names and numbers, file date range, or name of the government agency) that Archives staff members have entered. Using OCR scanning technologies and making the content of the records full-text searchable has been discussed at the Archives for many years, but no trial of how useful it could be had ever been conducted. We knew, of course, that OCR technology is in no way perfect. Even clear typewritten material is only likely to be interpreted at about 90 percent accuracy, and handwriting comes out as gobbledygook. OCR would work well for newer consignment lists but not so well for older, handwritten lists.

Second, we were excited about using the Hive as an opportunity to explore the possibilities of crowdsourcing. Using willing members of the public to correct the inaccuracies of OCR has been used in a few projects, notably the National Library of Australia's Newspapers project, now part of its online catalog Trove.[5] The Archives had some experience of crowdsourcing stories from the public to complement collection material—for instance, our 2009 project "Mapping Our Anzacs."[6] But we had never before asked for the public's assistance with transcription, so this was new territory. The public transcription work would support searchability of the consignment lists hosted on the Hive, but more importantly it would give the Archives valuable data it could add to the official descriptions on RecordSearch.

Our vision was that the Hive would become a site where people could search and view consignment lists, and if they chose, review the OCRed text and add corrections based on the images of the lists; in turn, the Archives would harvest the data entered by the public to create more record descriptions on RecordSearch. Instead of being reliant on only our own Archives staff to describe the collection, we would use technology (in the form of scanning and OCR) and crowdsourcing to bring more resources to the task.

In thinking about the design of our site, we were able to draw on some excellent work done analyzing the sorts of things that attract people to give up their time to assist a cultural institution improve its data quality. Rose Holley's checklist for successful crowdsourcing has become an industry standard, and we wanted to build on that framework.[7] We didn't want to fall into the trap of simply assuming that the public would want to participate just because the website was there. Although the public's work would result in more records being described from the content of the consignment lists, we weren't sure that people would even understand what a consignment list was. So another aspect of the Hive was the opportunity to assess people's motivation and interest in assisting the Archives. To accomplish this, we would also incorporate elements of "gamification" and see how including game-like elements for users into our site might help in creating an online community of volunteers and motivating individual contributors.

IMPLEMENTATION

The Archives' web developer took the website concept of crowdsourced transcription and ran with it. Wireframes were created and considered. Research was undertaken into other transcription crowdsourcing websites and approaches were adopted and expanded upon. The developer took the opportunity to include features that the Archives hadn't used in previous online projects. He built the site using Twitter bootstrap for the user interface components and leveraged the power of CSS3 to provide all the nice elements of the site such as rounded buttons. The jQuery framework was used for client-side interaction and ASP .NET 4.0 for server-side processing.

Trials were undertaken to find the best resolution for scanning for OCR output. Interestingly, it was found that 200 ppi (pixels per inch) was better than 300 ppi, as the higher resolution created too many "artifacts" that the OCR process interpreted as characters. At 200 ppi, and using the open-source Tesseract OCR engine, the scanned documents yielded about 80–90 percent accuracy, which was acceptable for this project. This finding was particularly welcome because our standard document scanning for RecordSearch was 200 ppi. This meant that staff wouldn't have to make any changes to their scanning equipment settings in order to participate.

It was decided that our initial pilot would be limited to scanning consignment lists in just one of our locations—our Brisbane office. This is a small office, and they were more easily able to redirect resources from scanning collection documents to scanning consignment lists. Uploading the consignment lists to the Hive required some new work processes to be created, and we wanted to get them right on a small scale first. We were unsure, too, about how many additional requests to access the records would result from this new and more detailed descriptive information being made available to the public, so keeping our first sample contained to one office seemed prudent.

We also decided that not all the lists at our Brisbane office would be scanned. Because the consignment lists come in a variety of formats and describe a wide range of records, we wanted to only select the lists that would be of most use to researchers. Working with Reading Room staff in our central office in Canberra, as well as staff from the Brisbane office, we developed these minimum standards:

- The list should include file titles with sufficient detail to assist the public in understanding what would be found in the file.
- Information about the arrangement and description of the material must be confirmed as adequate (series/consignments with known arrangement and description problems should be avoided).
- The list should be considered by Archives staff to cover accurately the records known to be in the consignment.
- The consignment described in the list should contain a sufficient amount of materials to ensure the scanning is an efficient use of time. Where only a small number of files are involved, staff data entry is preferred.
- The lists should meet certain legibility standards. The lists must be easily read, such as typed or neatly handwritten lists.

The lists also had to be for permanent records that were in the Archives' open-access period (the Archives' legislation has a 30-year—slowly becoming 20-year—closed period). In addition, they needed to cover a series where the materials had not already been described and for records that were in a suitable condition to be digitized if they were requested. Despite all of these conditions, there were a significant number of consignment lists from the Brisbane office that could be scanned—5,650 pages in total.

Due to staff concerns about the quality of information on the consignment lists, the Hive was built initially without the capability to harvest its information for RecordSearch. The assessment was made that we could at least investigate the other concepts first—harvesting the data would become a future goal if enough usable data were created to make it worthwhile.

The web developer's work and the Brisbane office work came together over the period of several months. When the site was ready, Brisbane started to load their lists. This process at first involved both some automation (as the OCR happened at time of loading) and some manual data entry of metadata specifying the government agency these records originated from, as well as the series description. With the initial set of lists posted, the first iteration of the Hive was ready for its first visitors in October 2012.

The Hive works in the following way. Once visitors arrive, he or she can begin participating right away, whether he or she chooses to create a user account or not, by selecting one of the consignment lists that appear randomly on the front page (see figure 1.1) and begin making corrections to that transcript. If users don't want to work on a randomly selected list, they have a couple of other ways to choose one. They may, for instance, want to select a list based on the level of OCR accuracy. Consignment

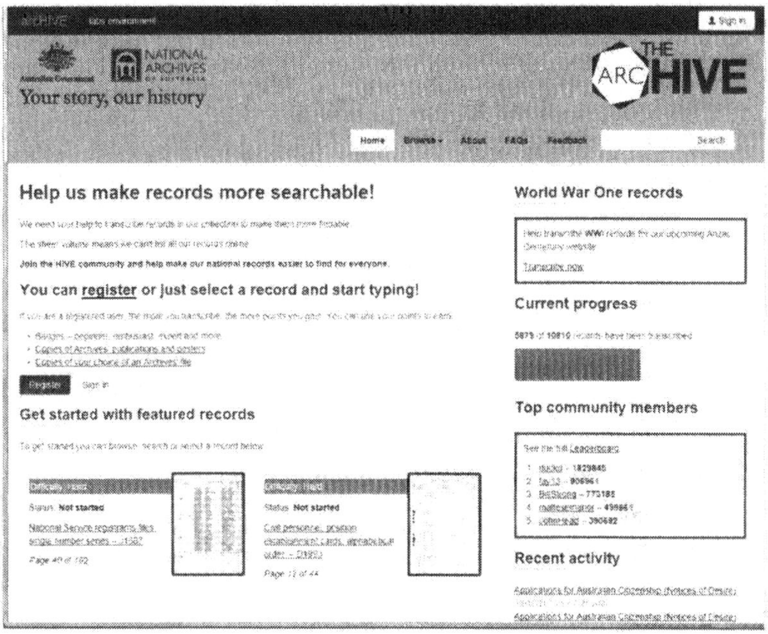

Figure 1.1. The front page of the Hive. There is a brief explanation about the site's purpose, and visitors can easily start reviewing scanned documents and correcting the OCRed text. They can track the overall progress of reviewed pages and also see who the top reviewers are.

lists, when loaded, are manually categorized as easy, medium, and hard, depending on how accurate the OCR process was. For example, a consignment list that was typewritten may have been 85 percent accurate, so it would require very little in the way of correction, and it would be ranked as easy. A handwritten list, on the other hand, would have been translated into a whole series of meaningless characters, and therefore would be rated as hard. Alternatively, users can search for particular areas of interest by using either a word search or by selecting to view lists from a particular government agency. The site's search works across all the metadata entered by staff as well as the raw OCR and transcribed data, so in theory, an interested researcher could come in and start looking for not only consignment lists but also individual files she hadn't been able to find on RecordSearch. If a researcher does find a record she is interested in, then the site has a function requesting a digitized copy of it.

Once a list has been selected, users are presented with a screen that shows both the scanned list and the OCR text (see figure 1.2). Users can correct part of a list and save it as an "in progress" status. Once they think review and correction is complete, that status can be upgraded to "completed." If another user disagrees with corrections or with a document's status, he or she can easily amend the work. The site saves all versions of the corrections, so no one's work is ever lost.

Motivation using gamification is also a feature. By introducing features such as point scoring, competition with others, and earning rewards, we hoped to make the Hive more interesting for participants. Visitors can elect to create a user account, in which case each of their keystrokes will start earning them points, and they start creating a longer-term relationship with the site, its goals, and hopefully with the Archives. These registered users are able to start earning badges as they experience different things on the site. For example, just signing up will get you a beginner badge, a few completed documents will get you an enthusiast badge, and so on. Users are also able to redeem their points for rewards. Archives posters and books are available, but the top reward is for an Archives file of the user's choice to be digitized and a hard copy sent to them, free of charge. Redeeming points will lose you your spot on the leaderboard, but it will earn you a badge.

The overall progress on the site is easily seen on the front page, where there is a bar chart showing how many consignment list pages have been loaded and how many have been completed. On the front page is also a

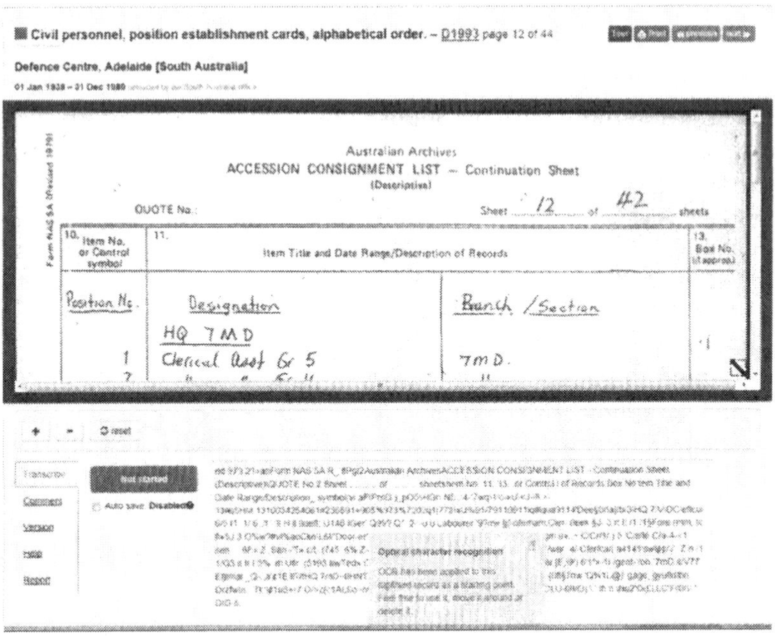

Figure 1.2. A typical consignment list page. At the top of the page is the metadata that has been entered by staff. Users see the original document on the top half of the page, and the field with the OCRed text is below. No one has started reviewing the raw text yet, and you can see the low accuracy that has been achieved by OCR of the handwriting on this document.

leaderboard that shows the top contributors and an area that shows the consignment lists most recently worked on. The work done is kept transparent to all users, so that it's easily seen who has been working on what lists.

RESULTS

The Hive was released first to Archives' staff and a couple of weeks later to the public. At that stage, there were only around 300 consignment list pages loaded. While it was an internal-only site, a large number of staff registered and worked on the lists. This was very valuable as our first user testing, and staff provided some feedback that resulted in a few little tweaks and fixes before the Hive went live to the public. Within a week of its public release, we had just over 100 more registered members and 160 completed lists. Within two weeks, all the lists that were categorized as "hard" had been completed. More Brisbane office staff were quickly trained to add content and started loading as fast as they could so that users wouldn't run out of work.

The Hive was promoted purely online via our website and also through the Archives' social media channels. There were quite a few tweets about the site, especially from the open government data community, with one person making the big claim that the site was "more fun than Angry Birds."[8]

At the time of writing, the site has now been running for 11 months. As of October 9, 2013, there are 9,391 pages of consignment lists available on the Hive, and 5,876 pages have been transcribed—representing approximately 150,000 files (see table 1.1).

The current loading rate is about 15–20 pages per day, or approximately 350–500 file descriptions. The Brisbane office has demonstrated that it takes about 21 hours to digitize and load enough pages to generate

Table 1.1. The progress made on the Hive in its first 11 months.

Date	Pages available	Pages transcribed	Approx. number of item descriptions
12 Dec 2012	1,918	756	19,000
23 Jan 2013	3,187	1,600	40,000
26 Mar 2013	4,786	2,683	67,000
22 April 2013	5,238	3,002	75,000
9 Jul 2013	7,075	4,245	106,000
8 Aug 2013	9,391	4,775	120,000
9 Oct 2013	10,810	5,876	150,000

20,000 descriptions: Traditionally that would be that office's entire annual data entry target. To date, the Brisbane office estimates they have spent a total of 160 hours—60 hours digitizing and 100 hours loading—on this project. Their work has yielded over 130,000 searchable descriptions. Using our traditional methods of collection description—staff pulling files from shelves and creating descriptions after examining each file—these 160 hours would have yielded only 3,000 to 3,500 descriptions for individual files.

It's one thing to know the volume of data the site has generated for the Archives, but of equal importance are considerations of how it works for our external audience. Statistics can tell us part of the story. There are on average between 30 and 50 visitors to the site every day, and they stay an average of eight minutes on the website. Visitors who come via our website seem to be more dedicated than people who reach the site in other ways, spending an average of 18 minutes on the Hive site. There is a small group of people who spend considerably longer periods of time there, however. In May 2013, we found that the top five users had contributed to just over half the total pages reviewed. Paul Hagon recently looked at this phenomenon of a small minority doing the bulk of the work in his crowdsourcing analysis of the National Library of Australia's Trove and he found that this pattern is common to many crowdsourcing sites.[9]

So what was actually motivating people to come to the site and continue their work? It's important for us to know, so that we can build on those strengths, increase audience numbers, and hopefully gain a larger core of dedicated transcribers. There certainly wasn't a particular topic that they gravitated toward, as is demonstrated when looking at the work of the most active users, and while most of them favor the hard records, others like working on the records ranked as medium and easy (see table 1.2).

Personal contact with some of the contributors gave us more insight into their motivations. In early 2013 we contacted the top 10 users to thank them for their work and to find out what they liked about the site. The most common answer was that they found the task interesting and were pleased to be undertaking work that was of assistance to the Archives. Assisting the Archives was seen to be of value. However, the details of their responses were as individual as the people themselves. One woman was using her work to get free copies of records about her father's service in World War II, so obviously she was finding the prizes motivating. Another reported that instead of finding the competitiveness of the leaderboard motivating, she found it embarrassing to see her name there and asked if there was any way we could remove it. One man wanted to see the number of descriptions that had been loaded to RecordSearch as a result of his work; only then would he really feel that he was contributing to something of value.

Table 1.2. Volume of pages completed, topics preferred, and primary level of difficulty selected for our top ten users (as of June 18, 2013).

User	Number of pages completed	Most frequent topic	Favored degree of difficulty
Duckd	412	Works/construction, Marine crews, Defense, Patents	Hard
Iamheywood	410	Works/construction, Bankruptcy, Defense, Royal Commission into Great Barrier Reef	Easy
Fay13	237	National Service passenger lists, Works/construction, Patents	Hard
Maltesemanor	181	Works/construction, Patents, Post office, Defense	Easy
BillStrong	473	Works/construction, Bankruptcy, RAAF, Patents, Crown solicitor, Passports	Hard
JohnHead	161	Commonwealth reporting service, Passenger lists, Works/construction	Medium
MarkR36	263	Bankruptcy, Aboriginal affairs, Works/construction, Industrial register	Hard

All of these responses have been useful and are informing our next steps with the Hive. This feedback also brought home the message that in order to continue to motivate people, we need to keep the Hive fresh, new, and responsive. We need to ensure that we keep loading new content to be transcribed, that we're acting upon feedback received. Dealing with the public on this site is like any relationship—we need to actively work at it to keep it going.

LESSONS LEARNED

Eleven months has been a good amount of time for us to assess the Hive and see how our choices have affected its success. Some of our expectations were met, and some have not come to pass. For example, while transcribers have taken to the site with enthusiasm, it has to some extent remained hidden to researchers who might find the content of interest. (Copies of only two files have been ordered from the website since its launch.) We are planning to create links from RecordSearch series information to the Hive consignment lists, so that any researcher who delves into series-level information will have access to the digitized consignment lists, listing all known files within that series.

We've also seen that users feel obligated to transcribe and correct the OCR for the documents exactly as they are presented. For example, if the record was in a table format they give it spacing so that it resembles a table. To address this we considered offering predefined templates for tables. However, doing this would mean including extra markup in the text that would eventually have to be stripped out when the data were loaded into RecordSearch, and so we decided that it was not worth the trouble. For the data to be harvested efficiently, this user-created formatting will have to be addressed.

We are also pleased that some of our initial choices seem to have been good ones. It appears that our efforts at gamification were a success. Even though, as noted, one person felt self-conscious about her achievements, others have given positive feedback about being able to see their progress through points and badges earned. We also want to show how many descriptions have now been added to RecordSearch as a result of the public's work.

While our first vision of the Hive was that we would begin feeding corrected OCR data back into the RecordSearch catalog right away, we have found that keeping the data harvest out of the initial scope of the pilot was a good move. It enabled the project to move forward more quickly than it would have been able to otherwise. Harvesting the information from the Hive to create new descriptions on RecordSearch is not going to be a completely automated process, but now that we've been able to see the quality of the data users are giving us, it looks as though the data can be entered with a minimum of manual handling. Certainly the loading processes at both ends of the Hive (loading the pages and downloading the final data) is looking quicker than our traditional process for creating descriptions of files. In addition, this experiment has led to some other thoughts around the Archives about collection-description innovations. For instance, there has been a suggestion that we could try creating OCR for the most recent consignment lists (which are all computer printouts) and then load that information directly to RecordSearch, without any manual verification by description archivists.

Our choice to not start out by harvesting the user-reviewed file descriptions from the Hive into RecordSearch was related to a larger issue, one that has been a learning experience for all of us at the Archives. When we first released the site to our staff, before its release for the public, it was clear that while some staff members had embraced the website's concept and were actively contributing, there was also some disquiet about involving the public in the task of describing the collection. There was concern about how this initiative would affect the staff members who were paid to enter the backlog of collection descriptions. Was it planned that this site would displace them and their work entirely? There was also wariness about allowing the public to participate in work that had, up until now, always been the responsibility of the Archives.

Allowing the public an active role in the description process was challenging for many. Could they be trusted? There have been projects in the past in which volunteers assisted with records description, but only one of those projects allowed the volunteers to actually enter the data (and even this project involved double-keying to ensure higher rates of accuracy). All of the previous projects involving volunteers were carefully supervised. The Hive was regarded as different because it allowed volunteers to work directly with description data. This wariness seems to me to be a vestige of the concept that the Archives has to maintain a "gatekeeper" role for its collection; that in being the authoritative source of Commonwealth government records, the Archives needs to insert itself firmly between the public and records.

The answer to these concerns about the quality of the data the public would provide came from the public users themselves. The people using the site showed obvious concern for the quality of the data by asking for guidance about how to transcribe correctly. As noted, when the scanned pages were laid out in table formats they wanted to replicate that in a free-text field. They asked us how we wanted abbreviations to be treated—should they be kept as is or spelled out? These were clearly a group of people very keen to do their best. This was further demonstrated when we saw that some users were monitoring and correcting other people's work.

While reassurance has come from seeing the quality of the data, our decision to make the site available first to staff through a series of demonstrations was valuable as well. Not only were the staff members able to test the site for us, but they could also voice concerns during the public forums we held about outsourcing work that had traditionally been their domain. Senior staff were able to use this as an opportunity to affirm that this site and the data generated from it were not intended to replace current staff. Rather, it was hoped that this new source of assistance could supplement current work practices. The past 11 months have demonstrated that this is indeed the case.

CONCLUSION

As we approach the one-year anniversary of the public launch of the Hive, staff continue to digitize and load consignment lists, and the public is transcribing material on a daily basis. At the time of writing, we have 563 registered users, and as the figures in table 1.1 show, our success in engaging the public in giving us accurate file-level descriptions is clear.

The Brisbane office has finished loading all of its consignment lists that meet the selection criteria, so now the Adelaide office has taken up the baton and is loading its material. Very soon we hope to see all of the Archives' offices loading consignment lists, including our main office in Canberra. In conjunction with this expansion of the project, we would like regional audiences to be able to easily identify consignment lists from their area, as consultation has shown people wanting to work on "their own" material.

We are also happy to see that staff who were initially dubious about the value of the project and whether crowdsourced data could be trusted are being won over. After seeing the Hive in action and doing their own analysis of the user-generated content, they're now satisfied that the work done by the public will complement the work done by their section of the Archives.

We are also starting to experiment with loading documents to the Hive that aren't consignment lists. We are now loading collection documents that we want to feature in a website to commemorate the centenary of World War I. This website will have documents with searchable content and will also feature the functionality of people being able to transcribe documents to make them more searchable. We're using the Hive to assess how people will transcribe them to help us design a more effective site for the World War I centenary. Already we've seen one user move away from consignment lists and dedicate himself entirely to these other documents.

Both these developments give us the opportunity—and the requirement—to make some improvements to the Hive site. We have seen the need to differentiate between images and OCR of records and images and OCR of the lists of records. This is a distinction that could be easily lost as we begin to post scans of actual records from the collections on the Hive site.

The relationship between the Hive and our collection database, RecordSearch, will also be made clearer. The titles in RecordSearch generated by the work of the Hive will have an indicator added to them to show that they come from user-generated data. Additionally, for all the series on RecordSearch that don't have file-level descriptions but have consignment lists on the Hive waiting for transcription, we will add a link from the description to the Hive, so that users are aware of this additional information (and the opportunity to contribute to sharing it). This should be of value to researchers who otherwise would not think to look elsewhere for information not included on RecordSearch.

The Hive has been running for less than 12 months, so is still very much in its trial stages. We are still learning about the project's potential to help the National Archives of Australia reach its target of having every one of its 40 million records described at the file or object level. However, it is enormously encouraging that we are getting enough usage and feedback from staff and the public to ensure that the project can grow and develop into a really useful tool, and help us achieve our goals for description, with the help of a generous crowd.

Zoë D'Arcy *is director of digital and online access at the National Archives of Australia.*

NOTES

1. "Crowdsourcing," Merriam-Webster, accessed October 18, 2013, www.merriam-webster.com/dictionary/crowdsourcing.

2. "NYPL Map Warper," New York Public Library, accessed October 18, 2013, http://maps.nypl.org/warper .

3. Zoë D'Arcy, "Creating the Labs Environment: Making Space for Innovation," in *Management: Innovative Practices in Archives and Special Collections*, ed. Kate Theimer (Lanham, Md.: Scarecrow Press, 2014). See also http://blogs.naa.gov.au/labs/.

4. Note that it is the practice in the National Archives of Australia to refer to this level of description as "item level." In our terminology, "items" are individual records in a format, such as files, volumes, maps, photographs, or sound recordings. For the convenience of North American readers, in this case study the terms "items" and "item-level" have been replaced with "files" and "file-level."

5. "Trove," National Library of Australia, accessed October 18, 2013, http://trove.nla.gov.au.

6. Tim Sherratt, "Bringing Life to Records: Mapping Our Anzacs at the National Archives of Australia," in *A Different Kind of Web*, ed. Kate Theimer (Chicago: Society of American Archivists, 2011), 128–38. See also http://mappingouranzacs.naa.gov.au.

7. Rose Holley, "Crowdsourcing: How and Why Should Libraries Do It?" *D-Lib Magazine*, 16, no. 3/4, March 2010, http://www.dlib.org/dlib/march10/holley/03holley.html.

8. Twitter, accessed October 18, 2013, https://twitter.com/maxious/status/263805228497915904.

9. Paul Hagon, "Crowdsourcing Behaviour," presentation March 4, 2013, accessed October 18, 2013, www.information-online.com.au/pdf/Tuesday_Concurrent_2_1125_Hagon.pdf.

TWO

More Than a <biogHist> Note

Early Experiences with Implementing EAC-CPF

Erin Faulder, Veronica Martzahl, and Eliot Wilczek,
Tufts University

It is easy to envision archival description standards merely as templates that only require archivists to fill in the blanks. Tufts University's Digital Collections and Archives (DCA) implementation of Encoded Archival Context for Corporate Bodies, Persons, and Families (EAC-CPF) demonstrates that implementing any standard requires thought, trade-offs, and careful decision making. By 2007, we were aware that our descriptive practices were limited when describing creators. Like many archives, our practice was to store creator information within the <biogHist> note of the appropriate collection's description. This was convenient but posed several problems. Although our <biogHist> notes for creators of manuscript collections, often individuals or families, were generally sufficient, a <biogHist> note did not support the complex descriptive needs of Tufts' institutional structure and the intricate relationships between university creators and collections. For university records, record creators evolve and change functions over time. Often a single office can be a creator of multiple collections. A single collection can also be associated with multiple creators. Tracking and maintaining this information was time consuming and prone to mistakes. As a result of these problems, the DCA's descriptions for institutional creators often went unwritten. We needed a better way to describe and manage record creator descriptions.

The DCA recognized that managing and describing our archival records in a fashion similar to the Australian series system, where collections and record groups are de-emphasized in favor of series that are tied to record creators, was an intellectual framework that could work for us.[1] Although we did not fully adopt the Australian series system, their work gave us an intellectual approach that led us to decouple description of record creators from collection descriptions. Ultimately, the DCA implemented EAC-CPF as our data-structure standard for these descriptions.[2] By decoupling creator description from collection description, the DCA was able to provide a richer depth and range of archival description with more efficient management. Using relationship ontologies, we can now link multiple creators to a single collection and a single creator to multiple collections without duplicating descriptive metadata. We can also relate creators to each other in order to provide greater structural information about the entities' relationships. Ultimately, this project both enhanced and transformed our description process.

In this case study, we discuss how the DCA implemented the EAC-CPF standard to describe the creators of its holdings of institutional university records and manuscript collections. We explore the array of local decisions we made while implementing this standard and the choices that led us to create our own tool for managing this information (CIDER), as well as benefits we have realized from separating the descriptions of record creators from descriptions of collections. As with any metadata standard, EAC-CPF is a tool that can help archives standardize, exchange, and scale their work. But standards do not remove the need for careful decision making by archivists. Implementing EAC-CPF forced us to reexamine our descriptive practices and assumptions about our work of describing creators and collections. The implementation process highlights problems we faced when applying abstract descriptive standards to local descriptive practice and discoveries of limitations in existing controlled vocabularies for functions and relationships. While other archives may not face these particular challenges when implementing creator descriptions, we hope that in presenting our experience we can offer a way of thinking about the broader planning considerations necessary for implementing EAC-CPF.

PLANNING

In January 2008, the DCA received a three-year Electronic Records Project grant from the National Historical Publications and Records Commissions (NHRPC) to expand our electronic records program.[3] The original scope of the grant focused on creating a tool for transferring electronic records. However, early in the grant we found ourselves in an unexpected, if wonderful, situation: A decision to restructure how that tool was developed meant we were both ahead of schedule and well under budget. With the additional time and resources available—and approval from our funding agency—we expanded our scope to look more closely at the creators and producers who would actually be using our transfer tool. In doing so, we realized that our creator descriptions for university record collections were minimal. We had a few histories written in our online Tufts Encyclopedia, but their static format made it difficult to update and reuse their descriptions in relation to our collection descriptions.[4] After consulting with NHPRC, we repurposed a portion of the funding to develop our documentation of record creators using EAC-CPF.

The NHPRC grant funding enabled us to hire a project archivist for 18 months, beginning in May 2009, to plan our initial implementation of records that described creators. During the planning process, we had to address three core questions:

- What elements should we use to describe record creators?
- What should be the system for managing the elements?
- What should be the data structure for disseminating the descriptions?

To answer the first question, we looked at our existing creator descriptions and identified common elements. Next we examined ISAAR (CPF) and DACS to review existing descriptive standards for creators.[5] From this review, we determined a preliminary core list of required and optional elements. This list continued to evolve throughout our implementation process as we considered how our descriptions would be managed, published, and accessed.

The second step was choosing a system that managed our elements and the data within them yet also supported easy dissemination of the complete record creator descriptions. The management environment needed to be flexible and extensible enough to handle large volumes of descriptive and relational information because we were separating creator and collection descriptions that existed in the same record. Managing relationships was an important requirement since links could exist between creators and collections, and among creators. Additionally, the DCA needed the data to be transformable so that they could be integrated and displayed into multiple collection descriptions through our EAD finding aids. Finally, we needed the description-to-access workflow to be seamless so we could focus resources on creating description rather than on generating finding aids.

Finding a system that balanced managing large amounts of information effectively and using that information efficiently led us through an iterative process of examining several solutions. Independently of the grant, the DCA was searching for a new collection management system and planning a redesign of our digital library. In light of our grant project work, our requirements for the collection management system grew to include the ability to accommodate record creator descriptions. We looked at open-source options—ICA-AtoM, Archivists' Toolkit, and Archon—but determined that none of them had both the record creator description capabilities and other system requirements that we were looking for. Commercial options were either beyond our budget or required too much customization to meet our needs.

As we reviewed archival collection management systems and were producing record creator descriptions for the grant project, we tried two interim ways to manage creator data. First, we attempted to manage the elements with a spreadsheet. That quickly became unwieldy due to the complex relationships among different types of records and the large, multiparagraph descriptions that were being forced into spreadsheet cells. There were also continuity problems since creators were being managed in the spreadsheet while collection information was managed in our existing collection management system. Additionally, crosswalking the metadata from the spreadsheet to a form that could be integrated with our EAD finding aids was cumbersome and unsatisfactory. Second, we tried to manage creator descriptions using a structure available in our existing commercial collection management system. However, we could not fully customize this structure to meet our requirements. It allowed us to export data flexibly, but we could not easily repeat fields or build complex relationships due to the system's limitations.

The timing of both projects was fortuitous. The DCA ultimately chose to hire a contractor to develop our own collection management database, Collection Information and Description Environment (CIDER). The grant project provided us an opportunity to define our new descriptive and functional needs, such as adding complex and repeatable relationships between creators and collections, which we then integrated into CIDER's design. We could customize this tool to meet our needs for scalable and transformable creator descriptions, yet it was still a less expensive option than commercial off-the-shelf products. For us, the benefits of having a system that fit our needs outweighed the challenges of designing and building it. Allowing our descriptive needs to drive the management tool selection, rather than allowing a tool to define and limit our descriptive practices, resulted in a satisfactory, scalable new approach for archival description.

The third step was to define a data structure that would effectively allow us to disseminate our creator descriptions. Fortunately, as we were approaching this step in August 2009, the Ad Hoc EAC Working Group released a draft of the EAC-CPF schema for public comment. It promised to provide a structural framework for the descriptive elements provided in ISAAR(CPF) in much the same way that EAD provides a framework for ISAD(G)[6] or DACS. The elements the DCA had previously defined to describe our creators were wholly represented in this schema. Additionally, the crosswalks to move these elements into a structured XML schema were well under way.[7] Using this standard, we could export our archival descriptions from CIDER into the EAD and EAC XML schemas for distribution and access through the Tufts digital library.

IMPLEMENTATION

When it came to implementing EAC-CPF, the bulk of our work revolved around how we would populate the new descriptive elements. In the same way that DACS provides guidance for the data elements in EAD but allows archives to determine local implementation, description in EAC-CPF requires local best practices.[8] In making these choices, we discovered descriptive limitations within certain elements (described in the following paragraphs) and the importance of defining why an archive wants to enhance creator descriptions.

Table 2.1 shows the complete list of descriptive elements that DCA employs and a brief explanation of our local implementation. As shown in the first column, some elements are repeatable and not all elements are required by the DCA.

There are additional descriptive elements available within the standard that the DCA chose not to use. For example, we felt that <place> was not a significant factor in defining the majority of our record creators since they would generally be listed as Medford, Massachusetts. However, we chose not to include this field as an auto-populated element because there are a few outliers, such as Edward R. Murrow, for which Medford would not be a useful or accurate descriptor. Although we could have manually changed these outliers, the cost of staff time to handle exceptions was considered too high for the benefit gained. Place is still described in the <biogHist> note but it is not a unique element.

Numerous elements within the EAC-CPF schema document the schema itself as well as the institution creating the data and track updates and modifications to the data. These include <maintenanceStatus>, <maintenanceAgency>, <languageDeclaration>, <conventionDeclaration>, and <maintenanceHistory>. At the DCA, we generate those elements by pulling from CIDER's audit trail or hard-coding them into the EAC-CPF export template. This allows us to focus our efforts on description, not data management.

Having defined the elements we planned to use, the next step was to write best practices and guidelines for our descriptive content. ISAAR(CPF) and DACS provided initial guidelines. However, our particular goals for this new descriptive practice and the process of implementation revealed that describing creators, as in describing collections, is not a simple matter of putting data into our elements. Below we explore the problems we encountered in describing individual people versus families, followed by a discussion of challenges in working with corporate bodies.

Table 2.1. Descriptive elements for the DCA implementation of EAC-CPF.

Element Required Status Repeatable Status	**Comments**
[recordId] Required Nonrepeatable	This element is part of the control portion of the EAC-CPF schema and it is essential to ensure that each record has a unique identifier. The DCA chose to use an alphanumeric identifier with no semantic value (RCR#####). This allowed us to ensure uniqueness while decoupling the link between creators and collections that ultimately would allow for many-to-many relationships between creators and collections and among creators.
[nameEntry] Required Nonrepeatable	This element indicates the authorized form of the name. Additional elements, which the DCA does not currently employ, can be nested underneath this element to parse out surname and forename, as well as provide information on the source of authorization (such as the Library of Congress Name Authority headings).
[nameEntryParallel] Optional Repeatable	This element allows for alternate forms of a name.
[entityType] Required Nonrepeatable	This element is used to determine if the creator is a person, family, or corporate body. This is a controlled vocabulary.
[existDates] Required Nonrepeatable	Additional elements allow for nesting greater detail within the [existDates] tag. These elements allow the DCA to parse our date ranges more cleanly by breaking the date into discreet units for start and end dates rather than providing a range in a single field. The DCA requires a start date for all entities, but the end date is optional in that an entity may be ongoing. For these cases, we select a check box in our collection management system for "ongoing" and this populates the schema at export with the word "present."
[biogHist] Required Nonrepeatable	This element has the option for a short abstract [abstract] element. Breaking this up into two sub-elements has allowed us flexibility in our utilization of the information. The [abstract], typically a summary of the [biogHist], can easily appear in related EAD records. The full history displays only in the EAC-CPF record, which is linked to the abstract in the EADs.
[structureOrGenealogy] Optional Nonrepeatable	The DCA primarily uses this element to describe corporate entities in more structured detail. These details might include list of directors or subdepartments. Occasionally, the DCA uses it to represent family relationships. Additional coding is needed within this element to ensure that the information displays properly, often by using the [list] tag.

[generalContext] Optional Nonrepeatable	Although the DCA has this element available, it is not actively being populated. It can be used for the inclusion of broader historical context beyond our institution useful to understand the environment of the record creator. For instance, at Tufts, the Jackson College for Women was established in 1910. The [generalContext] field could be used to provide more general information about women in higher education and the development of coeducation in America.
[source] Required Repeatable	This provides the source information for the record. The DCA currently creates the citation as a single text block due to the lack of subelements that would provide for flexible citation formatting on export.
[function] Optional Repeatable	Although the DCA has this element available, we are not currently using it due to a lack of a satisfactory controlled vocabulary for university functions.
[occupation] Optional Repeatable	This element can be extremely useful for the description of people who hold multiple positions within an institution over time. Subelements for dates are nested within this element.
[relations] Optional (strongly recommended) Repeatable	The DCA employs this element to describe the relationships among creators over time. We employ a controlled vocabulary based on Fedora Relationship Ontology to describe these relationships. The controlled vocabulary list requires that every relationship is categorized as one of the following: hierarchical, temporal, family, or associative.

People

People are relatively easy to describe. The rules in DACS and ISAAR(CPF) are clear about how to name them. The dates of their existence are finite and name changes are usually straightforward. Our existing collections' <biogHist> notes for individuals, previously coded in EAD, were more easily mapped to our EAC-CPF <biogHist> element than in cases of corporate bodies. The DCA's final rules for writing the biographical sketch of an individual creator of a collection are in textbox 2.1.

The DCA's descriptive policies endeavor to emphasize a person's relationship to Tufts. This strategic choice impacts our decisions about how to shape the narrative description of a person's life. We describe some creators more thoroughly than others because of the size of their collection and their relationship to Tufts. These are not simple choices, and some record creators present complex decisions about how much effort to put into their record and the best way to describe their relationship to Tufts. For example, poet John Holmes was a prominent member of the Tufts community and the creator of a significant collection in our holdings. His creator description emphasizes his relationship to Tufts rather than his place in 20th-century poetry. While we can describe his relation-

1. In the first paragraph, begin with:
    a. Individual's name
    b. Life dates in parentheses
    c. Association with Tufts (if applicable). If the person has had a long association, choose the most important role or roles that he or she has played.
2. In the second paragraph, give more general life information, including the following, if available:
    a. Full name, titles, married name(s), alias(es), pseudonym(s), and common or popular name(s) of persons.
    b. Birth date and location
    c. Death date and location
    d. Significant locations if essential for the biography and collection (e.g. Edward R. Murrow)
    e. Education
    f. Occupation, life, and activities
    g. Other work experience and important relationships
    h. Professional achievements
    i. Family information
    j. Other significant information.
3. If applicable, provide any extra information about his or her association with Tufts (e.g., anecdotes, trivia, etc.).
4. Conclude the narrative with a statement on the individual's death. If applicable, list any Tufts memorials associated with the individual (e.g., buildings or rooms that have been named for him or her).
5. Cite your sources in the Sources field.

Textbox 2.1. DCA guidelines for writing biographical notes for people and families.

ship to the Tufts community using our fairly simple relationship ontology, our disinclination to write entity descriptions for non-Tufts creators means we cannot easily describe his relationships to external people using the same strategy. Instead, we use a more traditional <biogHist> note to highlight his relationship to Robert Frost, as an example, and clarify the nuances of relationships he had with other creators in our holdings.

Families

When we have a family manuscript collection, we must decide when to make a single creator record for the whole family and when to create multiple personal creator records for individual family members. Both options are possible, so determining the preferred method is a matter of staff resources and descriptive needs. Sometimes the DCA has created multiple-person creator records for a single collection, such as in the case of the Rev. Thomas Whittemore family papers.[9] In this case, there are two record creator descriptions, linked together using relational metadata, for the two individuals whose materials are represented in the collection.[10] Other times, the DCA has decided to create a single record creator entry for the family, as in the case of the Etelman family papers.[11] The <bioGHist> note for the Etelman family creator record includes all members of the family whose material is in the collection. Their relationship to one another is represented in the <structureOrGenealogy> element rather than using linked records of each individual. In the case of the two Whittemore records, we had the staff resources to write two different record creator descriptions, and we anticipated that these records could be linked to more than one collection. In the case of the Etelman family, there was only going to be the single collection for which they were the creators so it seemed unnecessary to create multiple creator records, and the volume of materials contributed by each family member was relatively small and equal.

As we moved to using EAC-CPF records for all of our collections, our rationale for choosing whether to build creator records for every individual who is represented in the provenance of the collection or building one family record may come down to addressing the practical realities of staff time and descriptive impact. How much time is involved in researching and writing a full record for each individual versus the family as a whole? What is the potential benefit of having a record for an individual that can be associated with multiple collections? The power to create more granular many-to-many relationships among creators and collections makes writing individual personal records over family records appealing, but it is the more resource-intensive option and should be considered carefully.

Corporate Bodies

Corporate entities have proved more challenging when applying standards. The DCA's rules for writing the authoritative history of a corporate entity are in textbox 2.2. Our biggest challenge with the corporate record creators has been determining when to create a new record and when to append new information into an existing record. An institutional entity may change its name, its function, and its structural relationship to other entities many times. At what point is the entity so different from its original manifestation that it warrants a new descriptive record? In cases such as these, the guiding principle we have adopted is to create a new record when there is a change in the entity's function or structure. Generally, we have found that this kind of significant event is represented by a name change, which also acts as a signal to the Tufts community of the entity's new role. If a new record is created, we can link the two entities together through the relationship ontology and narrate the change in the history as necessary.

An example of this challenge is the description of the Tisch Library, the largest library at Tufts.[12] It primarily serves the School of Arts and Sciences and the School of Engineering. We chose to create a separate record for each previous iteration of the library and use the relationship ontology to link the records together. Tufts' first library in its own building was Eaton Library. When the library collection was moved to a new building in 1965, the name was changed to Wessell Library in honor of Tufts' president, Nils Y. Wessell. The name change from Wessell to Tisch Library in 1996 included not only an expansion of the building but also a realignment of the administrative structure of the Tufts libraries. The change in physical location in the first case and the change of functional oversight in the second, as well as accompanying name changes, led to the DCA's determination that individual records were warranted. The Tufts Libraries collection now links to both the Tisch and Wessell Library creator records and if, in the future, the library undergoes another transformation, we can link a new record creator to the collection.

Frequently entities change their names without a corresponding functional difference that would require a new record. This is often the case with academic departments and is one reason why we decided to impose a naming convention when creating institutional entity records. While Library of Congress Name Authorities exist for some of the larger units at Tufts, the vast majority of Tufts entities do not have their own record. The DCA first looked to follow the guidance of DACS, ISAAR(CPF), and

A complete history should include the following information in this order:

- Name—current and changes Include dates of changes when known and use the full name consistently throughout the description.
- Dates of founding and/or dissolution
- Changes in the main functions or activities and relations with other corporate bodies were significant
- Predecessor and successor bodies
- Names of significant people who worked in or headed the agency
- Other significant information not recorded elsewhere, such as publications, programs, and events
- In case of corporate or administrative amalgamations or mergers, name entities involved and summarize nature of amalgamation
- Cite your sources in the Sources field

Textbox 2.2. DCA guidelines for writing corporate body histories.

AACR2 in constructing authorized names. However, we found their advice difficult to implement without extensive research. A department might refer to itself as "Widgets Department" and as "Department of Widgets" within the same publication. Time constraints and recognizing the frequency with which departments changed their name but not necessarily their function played a role in our decision to impose a naming convention. Rather than determine the authorized names for each department on a case-by-case basis, the DCA chose to impose a format on the majority of names. Each unit would be "Unit type of name." For example, we have the "Department of History" and the "School of Engineering." This provides us with a consistent representation that aids in browsing the list of records. These kinds of local guidelines do not cover every eventuality and exceptions do exist. However, this overarching rule has allowed us to streamline the record creator description process and has shortened the time commitment needed in determining an authorized name for these kinds of organizations.

While implementing these guidelines, we have come across limitations in using specific elements. In particular, the <function> and <relations> elements sparked great enthusiasm during the planning phase, but we encountered problems with them during implementation. The DCA thought the <function> element would greatly enhance the corporate creator records. We envisioned this field serving as a point of aggregation where we could identify entities with similar functions, and compare and analyze the types of records they produced. The <relations> element offered us the opportunity to semantically link creators with each other, allowing us to produce a more accurate representation of departments, offices, and people at Tufts. For both <function> and <relations>, we first had to define the possible types of functions and relationships and then delineate the controlled vocabulary describing those elements. Ultimately, because we use a Fedora repository, we adapted Fedora's relationship ontology to describe creators' relationships to one another. However, neither the *Art & Architecture Thesaurus* nor the *Thesaurus for Use in College and University Archives* provided the ontology of function terms we needed. Ultimately we determined that while a controlled vocabulary of functions would be an extremely valuable resource to enhance our descriptions, we have not had time up to this point to undertake the necessary work to implement such a vocabulary.

RESULTS

Implementing EAC-CPF has given the DCA better information about the creators of our archival collections. By looking to the Australian series model and separating the descriptions of creators from collection descriptions, we are forced to spend more time describing our creators. Since creator descriptions are no longer subsumed within the collection description as a <biogHist> note but are instead displayed as their own record, the DCA must ensure that they are complete. This has changed our description workflow. Implementing EAC-CPF also allows us to display a navigable representation of the complex relationships that exist between creators and their records through our digital library.

The <relations> element is a powerful descriptive tool that allows us to describe our creators in new and useful ways. Take as an example a single administrator who was a member of the faculty at the medical school; had an appointment with an affiliated hospital; became a medical school dean for educational affairs, overseeing an administrative office within the medical school; and subsequently became an associate provost with oversight over several committees, university-wide initiatives, and offices. Her records, reflecting the multifaceted nature of her work at Tufts, are interspersed throughout multiple institutional collections; they are not pulled from the office papers into a personal collection or even necessarily separated into series within an office's collection. Rather than arrange her records to provide necessary archival context, we can create a record for the individual administrator as well as for each office with which she has a connection. These creator records can be associated together through the <relations> element, thereby representing her presence within multiple collections. In this way, we can present a network of relations between the person, the organizations, and the records to provide a more accurate picture of the material's provenance.

Because the DCA was able to integrate the development of our current collection management system and the redesign of our digital library with the development of our EAC-CPF elements and requirements, we have a smooth production workflow. We can now export descriptive metadata from CIDER as EAC-CPF records, ingest them into our repository, and display the enhanced archival context in our digital library. We can focus our time on writing the content because CIDER structures the data according to the EAC-CPF schema and exports an XML file with the push of a button. Within the digital library, the EAC-CPF and EAD displays have been designed to tie together seamlessly based on the relationships indicated in the records.[13] In future, we can incorporate changes to the EAD or EAC-CPF schemas within the CIDER export functionality. As a result of our planning, when an entity changes, we can generate updated creator descriptions and our system automatically incorporates those changes within the appropriate collection descriptions. We no longer have to expend resources to track down all the affected collections and change their <biogHist> notes.

LESSONS LEARNED

Transitioning from creating 50 published EAC-CPF records, as part of our NHPRC grant, to using these records in our daily operations, with over 900 skeletal records for manuscript and university record creators, has taught us a number of lessons. Decisions that made sense in the narrower context of the grant did not always scale up for our daily descriptive work.

Because the DCA implemented EAC-CPF as an expansion of a grant project that was creating a tool to transfer electronic records, our evaluation of why we wanted to implement EAC-CPF was heavily focused on describing future contributors of archival records. Our initial vision was to document all Tufts University entities; as a start, we created nearly 700 skeletal records. As part of the grant, we selected 50 creators to describe with full EAC-CPF records. As we produced those 50, we developed our best practices and policies that emphasized rich content and extensive linked relationships to other entities, some of whom did not have collection material in our holdings but who provided additional context. As we moved off the grant project, we shifted our efforts toward developing publishable EAC-CPF records for creators whose collection material the DCA already held so that we could make full descriptions of our collections available to our users. We have since revisited the initial best practices in light of the hundreds of skeletal records that still need to be researched, written, and linked to collections and entities. Although some record creator records have some existing description from the old <biogHist> notes in the EAD finding aids, most have little information beyond a name and date of existence.

Handling our descriptive backlog has required two approaches. First, for creators whose collections already have a <biogHist> note, we are transforming them into full creator records. However, we initially underestimated the time it would take to expand those notes into full creator records. The <biogHist> note from an EAD finding aid does not necessarily correlate seamlessly to the <biogHist> element in EAC. The text often needs revision and, due to our previous lack of prioritization of writing creator histories over collection scope notes, a considerable amount of research is still needed in order to meet our local rules for the minimum standard of publishable description. Second, we have moved the burden of creating new creator descriptions to our accessioning process. This keeps creator description forefront in our minds when we acquire new collection material. Although we may not write an extended narrative at the point of accessioning, we generate a minimum amount of information for all new accessions. If the accession adds to an existing collection with a skeletal record, it means dedicating time to writing the creator(s) descriptions for that collection.

Our descriptive backlog is a product of our limited descriptions before starting the project and an unanticipated shift in focus when moving from project to daily process. It is a result of us not clearly recognizing during our planning and early implementation phases the distinction between documenting Tufts University and describing our archival collections. At the time of creation of the skeletal records, we engaged in a proactive documentation approach. It provided us an interesting snapshot of the web of entities that made up Tufts University in 2010. However, there was little tangible payoff for our users because the skeletal records were insufficient to publish and historical university entities were not described. When we shifted to full production, a separate descriptive strategy emerged. As a result, the EAC-CPF records that are currently published and being written present a seemingly random set of entity descriptions because they are written based on processed collections rather than any systematic evaluation of the university.

The power of the <relations> element is still underutilized in our descriptive efforts. However, researching, documenting, and describing relationships take time. Investing this time naturally means spending less time completing other tasks. Every archive has to judge the value of the entity description and relationships they encode and assess if that time is the best investment of their resources. It is easy to be tempted by the dream of describing a virtually infinite set of relationships in a complex organization. Our initial documentation approach envisioned this sort of potential but vastly underestimated the resources necessary to accomplish it. In starting this kind of work, archives should take into account the payoff they anticipate this effort will provide instead of creating EAC-CPF records and relationships for their own sake. If the DCA were to undertake this implementation project again, we would focus on quality over quantity—selecting a few key, highly interrelated creators to start the process and creating full records for these entities. Rather than create hundreds of skeletal entity records, which are loosely linked together but have no other descriptive information, we would use the <structureOrGenealogy> element to document complex hierarchical structures. Future descriptive efforts could be spent replacing the <structureOrGenealogy> element with unique linked records as resources allowed.

Perhaps the most successful set of decisions we made concerned the elements we selected for our EAC-CPF records. This may not be as large of an undertaking for archives now that EAC-CPF is the standard. But our careful, early considerations about the elements necessary to describe our creators and conversations about how the creation-to-access workflow would work have paid off. The changes we made going into full-scale production were focused on levels of descriptions rather than modifying descriptive elements. Our minimum standard for creating a record have increased while our minimum standards for publishing a record has decreased in order to balance good description with the large number of records that need description. Future changes in the content standards, such as the second edition of DACS, can be easily reviewed and incorporated because we designed CIDER to be flexible to fit our descriptive needs.

While our initial creation of record creator descriptions underwent some rethinking in the scaling up to full production, our efforts to consider how our new metadata standards would be used from creation to access have been highly successful. Our choice to define descriptive needs with avenues for access in mind has meant that pushing record creator descriptions into an XML schema is speedy and scalable. Early attempts to manage information through spreadsheets and our old collection management system highlighted the importance of having a tool that fit our requirements in order to maintain descriptive integrity throughout the workflow. Developing a management system that fit our descriptive needs was a product of lucky timing and recognition of how one project could influence the outcome of another project. While creating a new management tool is not an approach every institution can undertake, allowing descriptive needs to guide system management tool decisions with the description-to-access workflow in mind has had enormous long-term productivity benefits.

CONCLUSION

Now that the DCA is using these descriptive practices in our daily workflows, we are looking at four ways of building on this initial work: (1) creating a denser network of entity records, (2) putting a greater emphasis on producing description through relationships rather than narratives, (3) undertaking a university documentation strategy to describe entities with no records in the archives, and (4) sharing EAC-CPF records with other archives.

We are currently focused on producing more EAC-CPF records for creators whose records are already present in our holdings. We are looking to generate enough records to reach a critical mass of connections between entities and collections with a minimum of at least one corresponding EAC-CPF record for every EAD record. Once we reach a sufficient descriptive density of relationships, we will look to use this network of connections as a core component of a new description strategy. The network of collections would allow us to describe an office, and by extension its records, through its relationships to other entities and its function. It is a new kind of descriptive approach that uses relationship and functional metadata displayed to users through queries of structured data rather than narrative description presented and navigated as blocks of text. This would allow us to display a dynamic finding aid that is generated from user queries on the relationships between entities and archival collections. A user's query on an entity or a function would produce a collection guide that describes the entity's role and relationship over time to the institution. A query on the Media Advocacy Board, which sponsors a number of Tufts student publications, would return collection material from 13 collections as well as the board's own archival material. As new accessions enter the collection and new relationships occur, we would update the EAC-CPF record and the query would return an updated finding aid. This supports our current exploration of linked data with our LiAM (Linked Archival Metadata) project.[14]

We are also considering the strategic implications of trying to more systematically document Tufts University. We anticipate that a key part of this work will be expanding our skeletal EAC-CPF records for Tufts departments, offices, and committees that do not necessarily have records in the archives. We attempted to do this as part of the initial grant project before turning away from the effort due to limited resources. Returning to this idea would be a significant shift in our priorities. It would mean placing a greater emphasis on documenting the institution, regardless of the current shape of our holdings, rather than focusing on enhancing the description of our archival collections. As discussed above, during our implementation work we did not make a clear distinction between a documentation and a description strategy. That lack of clarity left us with an abundance of skeletal records that we are now trying to figure how to best use.

Currently we only create relationships with other creators in our database. This reflects our Tufts-specific descriptive focus. However, we do have opportunities for building creator links beyond Tufts. For example, many of Tufts' past presidents have worked at multiple institutions over their careers and have records associated with these various organizations. Using linked data models, we could create a single, definitive EAC-CPF record for these past presidents that could be referenced and shared by all the archives that have related collections. The work could be done once for the benefit of all and could provide the core of records needed by the National Archival Authorities Cooperative to establish a national infrastructure of authority records. While our system is not currently configured to tap into this infrastructure or share our information with this project, CIDER has the flexibility to include this functionality in the future.

Erin Faulder *is archivist for digital collections and* ***Eliot Wilczek*** *is university records manager at Tufts University, Digital Collections and Archives. Until September 2013,* ***Veronica Martzahl*** *was records archivist at Tufts University, Digital Collections and Archives. She is now electronic records archivist at the Massachusetts Archives.*

NOTES

1. For a brief overview of the series system, see Adrian Cunningham, Laura Millar, and Barbara Reed, "Peter J. Scott and the Australian 'Series' System: Its Origins, Features, Rationale, Impact and Continuing Relevance," presented at the International Congress on Archives, Brisbane, Australia: International Council on Archives, 2012, accessed August 15, 2013, www.ica2012.com/files/pdf/Full%20papers%20upload/ica12Final00414.pdf.

2. See the EAC-CPF tag library for a more complete description of the project's background and aims. Encoded Archival Context Working Group of the Society of American Archivists and the Staatsbibliothek zu Berlin, "Encoded Archival Context—Corporate Bodies, Persons, and Families (EAC-CPF) Tag Library," University of Virginia, Institute for Advance Technology in the Humanities, accessed October 7, 2013, www3.iath.virginia.edu/eac/cpf/tagLibrary/cpfTagLibrary.html#d1e57.

3. National Historical Publications and Records Commission Electronic Records Program Expansion Project grant (RE10005-08), Digital Collections and Archives, Tufts University, "TAPER: Tufts Accessioning Program for Electronic Records," Digital Collections and Archives, accessed August 15, 2013, http://sites.tufts.edu/dca/about-us/research-initiatives/taper-tufts-accessioning-program-for-electronic-records/.

4. Digital Collections and Archives, Tufts University, "Concise Encyclopedia of Tufts History," Digital Collections and Archives, accessed October 7, 2013, http://hdl.handle.net/10427/14829.

5. For a fuller description of the International Standard Archival Authority Record for Corporate Bodies, Persons and Families [ISAAR(CPF)], see the International Council on Archives, accessed October 7, 2013, www.ica.org/?lid=10203.

6. For a fuller description of the General International Standard Archival Description, 2nd ed., see the International Council on Archives, accessed October 7, 2013, www.ica.org/?lid=10207.

7. For an example of an ISAAR(CPF) to EAC crosswalk that was available at the time of our grant work, see the University of Virginia, Institute for Advance Technology in the Humanities website, accessed August 12, 2013, www3.iath.virginia.edu/eac/documentation/ISAAR2EACbeta.html.

8. The second edition of DACS addresses some of the issues we had to solve for ourselves.

9. Digital Collections and Archives, Tufts University, "Rev. Thomas Whittemore family papers," Digital Collections and Archives, accessed October 7, 2013, http://dl.tufts.edu/catalog/ead/tufts:UA069.001.DO.MS178.

10. Digital Collections and Archives, Tufts University, "Reverend Thomas Whittemore EAC-CPF Record," Digital Collections and Archives, accessed October 7, 2013, http://dl.tufts.edu/catalog/tufts:RCR00926; Digital Collections and Archives, Tufts University, "Thomas Whittemore EAC-CPF Record," Digital Collections and Archives, accessed October 7, 2013, http://dl.tufts.edu/catalog/tufts:RCR00927.

11. Digital Collections and Archives, Tufts University, "Etelman Family Papers," Digital Collections and Archives, accessed October 7, 2013, http://dl.tufts.edu/catalog/ead/tufts:UA069.001.DO.MS204.

12. Digital Collections and Archives, Tufts University, "Tisch Library EAC-CPF Record," Digital Collections and Archives, accessed August 12, 2013, http://dl.tufts.edu/catalog/tufts:RCR00579.

13. For an example of integrated EAD and EAC records, see Digital Collections and Archives, Tufts University, "Ellen L. Lutz Papers," Digital Collections and Archives, accessed August 12, 2013, http://dl.tufts.edu/catalog/ead/tufts:UA069.001.DO.MS177 and the accompanying Ellen L. Lutz creator record, accessed August 12, 2013, http://dl.tufts.edu/catalog/tufts:RCR00925.

14. Institute for Museum and Library Services National Leadership planning grant, Digital Collections and Archives, Tufts University, "LiAM: Linked Archival Metadata," Digital Collections and Archives, accessed August 15, 2013, http://sites.tufts.edu/liam.

THREE

Creating Access and Establishing Control

Conducting a Comprehensive Survey to Reveal a Hidden Repository

Matthew B. Gorham and Chela Scott Weber,
Brooklyn Historical Society

Many archival repositories face significant backlogs over which they have very little, or no, intellectual or physical control. These backlogs cause a variety of issues across the continuum of archival work, from collections management to public services and everything in between. Fortunately, we have talented colleagues who have faced similar problems and have developed a variety of tools and techniques from which we can draw and adapt in order to address the unique circumstances of our individual situations. This chapter discusses the backlog at the Brooklyn Historical Society (BHS), the way it affected the institution, and the survey and minimal processing project that we undertook to try to address it. We discuss how we approached the survey and minimal processing as well as the different models we adapted to fit our needs, and we reflect on the successes and challenges within the project.

Brooklyn Historical Society is an urban history center dedicated to preserving and encouraging the study of the history of the borough of Brooklyn in New York City.[1] The Othmer Library at BHS is a research library open to the public that serves a diverse range of users, including K–12 students and educators; undergraduates, graduate students, and university faculty; amateur and professional genealogists; enthusiasts of the history of Brooklyn and locals interested in the history of their home or neighborhood; and artists, authors, and documentarians. In addition to outside researchers, the library plays a core role in supporting the education and exhibit programs of the larger institution.

Collections at the BHS library include archive and manuscript, image, oral history, and special collection holdings documenting the history of Brooklyn and Long Island from the time of European settlement in the 1640s to the present day. Supporting these collections is a small staff, with three full-time professional library positions in the annual budget: a librarian, an archivist, and a library director (who, at the time of this project, was Chela Scott Weber). Anywhere from two to five additional, full-time, soft-money-funded professional and support positions usually augment the staff on a fluctuating basis depending on current projects. The library partners with New York University to catalog into their integrated library system and enable resource discovery through their online catalog, BobCat, and their finding aid discovery portal.

BHS has been building its archival collections since its founding in 1863. By 2005, the archives had reached a size of 2,500 linear feet organized into approximately 1,608 individual collections. The history of collections management varied widely over this almost one-and-a-half-century span, and practice had not been consistently documented. There had been numerous numbering systems for accessioning and collection identification over time; neither the periods of use nor the relationships between the systems were clear. Many collections had been pulled apart according to format, so that photographs, maps, prints and other artworks, and textual materials that had been donated together were treated as distinct collections. These separations were not consistently recorded, thus destroying both original order and making provenance difficult to reestablish. Even when collections had not been pulled apart, provenance and custodial history for archival materials brought in before the 1970s were either not recorded in any consistent manner, or were but these records had been lost. Additionally, arrangement and descriptive work performed on these collections was inconsistent: Some were fully physically processed and described to the folder level; some were partially or entirely physically processed and rehoused but had little or no accompanying descriptive information; and others were entirely unprocessed with no descriptive information at all.

These issues were exacerbated by a protracted period of closure of the library from 1998 to 2005, during a building renovation that had gone significantly over budget and schedule. During this period, library staffing had been varied and sparse. By the time the library reopened to the public in 2005, there were no library staff members left from the pre-renovation period, causing a significant gap in institutional memory. There were a number of different descriptive representations of the collections from different eras—a card catalog of manuscript collections from the early to mid-1900s, a published book of records from a borough-wide historical document inventory from the 1980s, and various paper and electronic finding aids of different levels of detail and accuracy. However, we often found it difficult to match these descriptions to the physical collections they described. Other than a Microsoft Access database with location and very skeletal descriptive information, there was no structured data about archival collections.

Our own frustration in understanding our collections was matched, if not exceeded, by that of our patrons. In 2008, our website only displayed finding aids for our five largest collections.[2] The rest of the collections were effectively hidden, but there was still significant researcher interest in using our holdings. Library staff had to mediate almost all resource discovery through reference interactions, which was a slow and frustrating process given our array of inefficient, incomplete, and obsolete legacy descriptive tools. Our queue of remote reference requests was more than our small staff could handle, and often had a two-month or longer response time. Requests for reuse and publication were particularly onerous, as assessing rights in this situation was extremely time consuming and cumbersome.

It was clear that we needed a plan to establish both physical and intellectual control of our collections and that the solution had to include a vehicle to provide researchers unmediated, online discovery of the collections. Our solution was a comprehensive project to survey and describe the entirety of our archival holdings, which was designed to provide a baseline of physical and intellectual control across all collections; quantitative data on holdings to be used as a tool for future decision making; standardized descriptive practice; and a clean, normalized set of descriptive data about holdings that could be pushed out to multiple online discovery systems to better serve researchers and encourage collection use. In this case study, we describe our process of designing a project to address the problems discussed above, how our project was carried out, and offer advice in hindsight for colleagues who might be considering a similar project or facing similar challenges in their own repositories.

PLANNING

Though the library faced a challenging situation, it did have the advantage of understanding and support from its parent institution. In the BHS 2007–2011 strategic plan, the institution had recognized collections care as a crucial issue and identified as a main goal to: "Manage our historic resources at the highest professional standards, providing protection and care for the collections while making them available and useful to the community."[3] Within the library, we responded to the strategic plan by identifying concrete initiatives that would move us toward fulfilling this institutional goal but were specific to our collections and our most pressing needs. These were to:

- Implement Archivists' Toolkit (AT) to bring all description, location, and accession information together into one place and create structured descriptive data
- Understand and plan for collection conservation and preservation needs
- Assess provenance and intellectual property ownership of all collection
- Reassociate photographs and other formats separated from textual collection
- Provide online access to collection-level description, at minimum, for all collections

When we began thinking about how to address these initiatives, we knew we wanted to think holistically about our approach and try to design a project that would address most, or preferably all, initiatives rather than each one individually or sequentially. Looking carefully at our challenges and identified initiatives, we began to think of our backlog not as unprocessed collections but as "unaccessioned" collections, because the groundwork of initial physical and intellectual control that is the goal of accessioning had not been established for our holdings. Without this foundation, all our other functions—reference, collections management, rights assessment, collection development, and so forth—were a far heavier load than they ought to have been. Accordingly, in designing a project to address these initiatives, we needed to re-create this foundation with a project that looked much more like an ideal and robust accessioning workflow rather than a traditional processing project. In order to do this, we felt strongly that the whole of the archival collections needed to be addressed rather than just a subsection of them, to ensure access across the totality of holdings and so that we could begin to understand what we held in its entirety in order to best prioritize and address future needs.

Our ultimate plan was inspired by these needs and a variety of recent work and publications by peer institutions and colleagues. The survey methodology developed at the Historical Society of Pennsylvania[4] and later adapted for the full Philadelphia Area Consortium of Special Collections Libraries (PACSCL) offered an excellent model to assess our current levels of physical and intellectual control and the physical state of collections.[5] Christine Weideman's thinking about "accessioning as processing," or putting significant effort into public-facing descriptive surrogates at the point of accession, offered an example of baseline description that could be used for access and discovery.[6] We also drew inspiration from Robert S. Cox's reframing of More Product Less Process (MPLP),[7] urging archivists to think beyond the minimum necessary and instead think in terms of the maximum possible in our descriptive work, both immediately and into the future.[8] We would seek to develop a thoughtful, user-centered approach to our baseline descriptive records and implement our systems in such a way that the work could be easily iterated upon later. We decided that a survey following the PACSCL model, along with creation of robust collection-level description across our holdings, would allow us to act in the short term to address discovery needs—and also to plan for the long term—by designing a project that would create metadata for and knowledge about the collections that would serve as this foundation to be built upon in future work. The survey data and baseline descriptive records, combined with AT implementation, strong documentation of descriptive practice, and consistent application of internal and national descriptive standards, would allow us to build a solid descriptive infrastructure, responsible collection management practice, and a decision-making and priority-building infrastructure for the future.

Once the general approach and goals were established, we sought to put together a project plan and schedule. We were particularly concerned with developing a realistic timeline for the project and struggled with how to estimate the time it would take to do the survey and description work. We could not simply factor the linear feet involved and multiply them by an estimated hourly rate of processing time. We needed to also consider the total number of collections, how long we thought gathering survey ratings information would take, how long doing descriptive work for each individual collection would take, and how much time and effort might be involved in reuniting previously separated materials. We also wanted to add a modest but realistic buffer to take into account the nature of hidden collections and the knowledge that there could be any number of unplanned scenarios that might knock us off schedule.

We were also challenged by how to staff the project. The PACSCL methodology called for the survey work to be carried out in teams of two. Feedback we got from others who had used this methodology was that the team approach was valuable for the consistent application of survey ratings and also seemed to help keep morale high during some of the more tedious parts of the work. We thought two survey teams would be necessary to carry out the work in a condensed time frame but were unsure if they all needed to be full-time, professional staff. The grant programs from which we were planning to request funding put an emphasis on efficiency and on using a full range of professional, paraprofessional, student, and volunteer labor as appropriate to the tasks of the project. We felt strongly that we needed a full-time, professional archivist to lead the project but decided it was appropriate to employ paraprofessionals for the rest of the members of the survey team. This decision was influenced by our location in the New York City area, where there are six library or archival graduate programs. We felt confident that we would be able to find qualified, engaged students in the midst of their master's programs who would be qualified for these positions and learn much through their participation in the project. We also hoped it might increase our likelihood of securing funding.

Ultimately, we came up with a two-and-a-half-year project, carried out by four project staff members: a full-time archivist who would lead the survey team and work through the duration of the project, and three part-time paraprofessional archives technicians who would work for the 18 months of the project devoted to carrying out the survey and descriptive activities. The project plan was divided into three parts. Phase 1 was a six-month planning stage, in which we would hire and train the project archivist, who would begin work on documentation for carrying out the survey, gather all legacy description and accession information to be consulted in the survey, and create training materials for the rest of the team. At the end of this phase, we would hire and train our three part-time archives technicians. During Phase 2, all of the survey and description work was to be completed by the survey team, over a period of 18 months. Phase 3 was to be devoted to a wrap-up of the descriptive work, with the project archivist working to export descriptive data from the AT to our multiple discovery systems. During this phase, we would also work with a contract programmer to develop a WordPress plug-in to be able to programmatically transform MARCXML exported from the AT and display it in our WordPress-based "catablog," Emma.[9]

Given the size of the library staff and the institutional budget, we had to seek outside funding for the project. This is another reason the PACSCL methodology was attractive, as a number of similar projects at peer institutions based upon the PACSCL model had recently been funded through major archival grant programs. Our project was ultimately funded through a Council on Library and Information Resources Hidden Collections grant, with additional funding from the Gladys Krieble Delmas Foundation.

IMPLEMENTATION

The project commenced in January 2010 with the hiring of the project archivist, Matthew Gorham. From January to April, he carried out preliminary work that was necessary before the survey could begin in earnest. The first major task was to gather all of the available descriptive and accession paperwork for the collections to be surveyed. Because previous processing and description work for these collections was inconsistent, the available records varied widely and included everything from detailed, folder-level finding aids to box inventories and typed index cards in a card catalog. All of the collections had an accompanying paper accession file, again containing varying amounts of information about the provenance and custodial history of the collection. In addition to this paper trail, there was basic legacy descriptive information in a Microsoft Access database, which Matthew mapped and imported into the AT Accessions Module.

Matthew also concurrently developed the survey ratings instrument and composed training manuals for minimal arrangement and description, and operation of the AT, using documentation from the PACSCL survey project as the point of reference.[10] The PACSCL survey ratings instrument requires survey teams to rate each collection on five Likert scales: Physical Condition, Physical Access, Quality of Housing, Intellectual Access, and Research Value. In addition to these, we developed two new categories for the survey of BHS's collections: Exhibition Value and Completeness of Accession Records (see table 3.1). These latter categories were deemed crucial to support BHS's institutional mission as a museum, as well as to help clarify long-standing confusion over provenance and legal ownership of collections, respectively. In mid-May, Patricia Glowinski, Nicholas Pavlik, and Weatherly Stephan were hired as archives technicians. They spent approximately two weeks training in the use of the AT, reviewing project training manuals, familiarizing themselves with the library and archival collections, and reading up on Brooklyn and New York City history.

Table 3.1. BHS survey ratings table.

	5	4	3	2	1
Physical Condition	• Excellent • Little damage • No expectation of further deterioration	• Very good • Little damage • Some further deterioration possible	• Good • Expected deterioration • Some further deterioration possible	• Fair • Somewhat worse than expected • Some further deterioration possible	• Poor • Significant damage/ deterioration • Collection difficult to use
Physical Access	• Full, orderly arrangement to appropriate level (i.e., series, subseries, file) • Single volumes are orderly and indexed	• Partial, somewhat orderly arrangement • Generally good order within files • Single volumes are orderly	• Rough arrangement • Series and files not fully established • Significant work required of researchers to locate certain document types	• Partial/ superficial arrangement • Nonstandard housing and/or labeling • Use discouraged except with staff assistance	• Totally unarranged • Completely inaccessible to researcher
Quality of Housing	• All housing is acid-free and in good condition • Containers and enclosures are reasonable filled • All containers and enclosures are the correct size and type for the materials they house	• Some housing is acid-free and in good condition • Most containers and enclosures are reasonably filled with materials • Most containers and enclosures are the correct size and type	• Housed in non-archival containers and enclosures in good condition • Most containers and enclosures are reasonably filled • Most containers and enclosures are the correct size and type	• Housed in non-archival containers and enclosures • Housing is filled beyond reasonable capacity • Most of the housing is not appropriate for the type of materials	• Housed in non-archival containers and enclosures • Some items might be loose on the shelf • Majority of materials not in proper housing or in overstuffed/ understuffed housing

		for the materials they house		contained inside	
Research Value	Interest: Very High Quality of Documentation: Very Rich	Interest: High Quality of Documentation: Rich	Interest: Moderate Quality of Documentation: Moderately Rich	Interest: Slight Quality of Documentation: Incidentally Valuable	Interest: Negligible Quality of Documentation: Slight
Intellectual Access	Excellent access: • Online EAD finding aid available • MARC record in an OPAC available • Offline descriptive tool available	Good access: • Offline finding aid available • MARC record in an OPAC available	Fair access: • The available finding aid is substandard or is unavailable • MARC record in an OPAC available • An offline descriptive tool provides sufficient access due to the small size of the collection	Poor access: • The available finding aid is substandard or is unavailable • No MARC record available or the collection is too large and complex for it to provide sufficient access • Offline descriptive tools provide insufficient access	No access: • Internal documentation such as a donor/control file or brief accession record is the only descriptive tool available
Completeness of Accession Record	• Unique accession # assigned to collection • Deed of gift or bill of sale present • Correspondence, research materials, or other supporting documents present	• Unique accession # assigned to collection • No deed of gift, or other documentation indicating ownership	• Unique accession # assigned to collection • Supporting documentation is spotty and provides little or no provenance	• Collection may or may not have an assigned unique accession # • No legal documentation, donor contact info, supporting	• The collection has no assigned unique accession # • An accession file may or may not exist • If the file exists, it only lists the donor's name and no

	• Basic bibliographic/ inventory info present • Separation of materials documentation present (if applicable)	• Some supporting documentation present • Incomplete bibliographic / inventory information	or ownership info • Incomplete bibliographic / inventory information	documentation, that clearly establishes provenance or ownership • Bibliogrpahic/ inventory info either very poor or nonexistent	accession date • Legal or supporting documentation, bibliographic/ inventory info, etc. are not available
Exhibition Value	• Items have great visual/aesthetic appeal • Materials in excellent physical condition • Subjects documented would have a wide audience appeal • Materials are unique, historically significant, and/or document a famous person, place, etc.	• Materials have above-average visual/aesthetic appeal • Materials are in good physical condition • Materials would appeal to a wide audience, but are not necessarily unique and are somewhat historically significant	• Materials have average visual/ aesthetic appeal • Materials are moderately historically significant and are not terribly unique • Materials of interest to a limited audience • Materials in average physical condition	• Materials have very little visual/ aesthetic appeal • Materials have very limited audience appeal • Materials show little historical significance and are not unique • Materials in fair-to-poor physical condition	• Materials have no visual/aesthetic appeal • Subject matter of the materials would be of no interest to a wide audience • Materials are in very poor physical condition

As we neared the official start of the survey phase, our biggest question was where to begin. The collection size ranged from single documents to upwards of 50–100 linear feet, and varied widely in material type and degree of prior processing and description work performed. There was also the complication of the significant body of materials of the same provenance that had been separated and treated as distinct and unrelated collections. This issue in particular greatly affected our treatment of the aforementioned paper accession files and led to a major modification of the original project plan. We had originally planned to consult the paper accession records throughout the project as we surveyed each individual collection. However, it became increasingly evident that the information contained in these records would be key to bringing the separated collections back together and that reuniting them at the outset of the project would clear up most lingering questions of provenance and leave us with a clear set of discreet collections to survey and describe. Thus we altered the plan, transcribing all of the more than 3,000 accession records into the AT before starting the survey, including adding name authority headings for donors and creators. With the data in structured format in the AT, we were able to easily identify collections with like creators and more efficiently identify accessions that should be described together. Though long and tedious, this task proved to be entirely worthwhile, and we believe it saved significant time, effort, and frustration in the remaining portion of the project.

With this last preparatory step complete, we began the physical survey of the collections. Based on the compiled legacy data, we classified the collections into broad subgroups and tackled them in the following order:

1. Collections comprised of separated accessions that needed to be rejoined
2. Manuscript collections measuring 0.5 linear feet and larger
3. Photographic collections
4. Manuscript collections measuring smaller than 0.5 linear feet

Each project staff member used a laptop computer to record his or her work in the AT, and each team of two used a modular laptop desk to survey the collections in the stacks. In a typical week, we spent mornings working in our teams of two, physically examining each collection; assessing available descriptive tools and accession paperwork; coming to a consensus on ratings for the seven Likert-scale categories; and writing supporting notes on our decision-making process as needed. Survey ratings were recorded in the AT Assessment Module. In the afternoons, we divvied up between survey team partners the collections we had just surveyed and each person composed descriptive records for his or her assigned collections in the AT Resource Module.

To ensure consistent description practices, we utilized *Describing Archives: A Content Standard (DACS)*. We wrote, or revised when available, scope and content notes, historical or biographical notes, and provenance notes. We assigned Library of Congress subject and name headings and Getty Art & Architecture Thesaurus genre headings. We also recorded access restrictions as well as copyright and use restriction information. We described the majority of holdings at the collection level, though select collections were described at the series level due to their large size or because previous processing or description work made this information readily available for entry in the AT. Project work was supervised by the archivist, Julie May, and by Chela, as library director, through regular meetings with Matthew individually and with the full survey team. At the outset of the survey, we used these full-team meetings to do regular peer review of descriptive records, to discuss descriptive work, and to check in on the overall progress of the project. Though we were initially concerned that these sessions might prove too time consuming, they in fact led to many fruitful discussions about our approach to description that, in hindsight, were very important to the success of the project.

One of the more interesting and unexpected challenges in this phase of the project was our initially steep minimal description learning curve. All of the project team members were very early career archivists and were in the midst of, or had recently completed, MLIS degrees at universities where traditional, folder-level arrangement and description was the curricular standard, and MPLP was a set of ideas we spent perhaps one class period or less learning about and discussing. Early on, it became evident that we were often spending too much time writing overly long and detailed descriptive records and that we would need to significantly tighten up our approach if we wanted to complete the survey on time. Through these team meetings, for example, we decided that biographical, historical, and scope and content notes should be kept to one succinct paragraph apiece and that a single summary abstract could suffice in lieu of these two notes for very small collections or when otherwise appropriate.

These meetings also entailed many discussions on just what our minimal description should contain and included discussion of BHS's users—the types of researchers we needed to cater our description to, the types of reference questions they typically asked, and the types of material and subject matters they sought in our collections. These conversations benefited greatly from participation from both project staff and Chela and Julie, who, as long-term staff, knew the BHS user population well and helped us steer our questions about approach back to considerations about how to best serve discovery and use for the BHS patron base. For example, we knew that patrons regularly asked for collections documenting specific Brooklyn neighborhoods, so we decided that, as a rule, we would always include the names of neighborhood(s) represented in a collection in our description, and we created local subject headings for neighborhoods that had no Library of Congress authorized heading. Similarly, we worked very hard to make relevant materials discoverable by BHS's significant genealogist user base. Interestingly, policy decisions in this area involved not only highlighting materials in a collection that would be of interest to genealogists but also sometimes pointing out the types of relevant materials that were *not* present in a collection. In our experience, BHS genealogy researchers most commonly sought out birth, marriage, baptism, and death records. We also knew that with collection-level records, it might not be clear just what was in the full collection. By specifying that a collection of family papers or church records *didn't* include such records, we hoped to save reference staff time and spare users the frustration of encountering dead-ends in their research.

When project staff meetings resulted in consensus decisions on new or revised arrangement and description policies, we recorded them in existing manuals along with the date on which the decision was made to ensure adherence to the policy going forward. As the project progressed, we gradually scaled these meetings back. As we honed our arrangement and description skills and became more efficient at our work, the meetings and need for supervision gradually became less necessary, and the increasingly fast pace at which we produced descriptive records did ultimately render the formal peer-review process much too time consuming. The weekly meetings continued over the first few months of the project, after which they were scaled back to biweekly meetings, and during the last couple of months we checked in only on an as-needed basis and performed only basic spot checks of each other's descriptive records. The survey was successfully completed in October 2011, after which the archives technicians departed BHS and Matthew set to work exporting MARC and EAD records from the AT and publishing to the various discovery portals.

RESULTS

The survey project was completed successfully in May 2012 within its two-and-a-half-year timeline. In all, we completed descriptive records for 1,411 individual collections and published them online, which accomplished the goal of gaining control over our hidden collection backlog. EAD finding aids were published to the NYU consortial finding aid portal, which enables full-text search of records as well as discoverability via an Internet search engine. MARC records published in NYU's BobCat online public access catalog (OPAC) provide discoverability alongside BHS's book and map collections and are also exported to WorldCat. MARC records were also published to Emma, the BHS catablog, which offers several unique advantages. Because it is built using the WordPress open-source blogging platform, Emma provides BHS with a low-cost, flexible, and customizable option for publishing collection information to the web that is indexed by Internet search engines, allows for integration with Google Analytics so that use statistics can be tracked, and allows BHS a level of local control that the interfaces available through the consortial relationship with NYU do not. Archival collections can be searched or browsed in Emma alongside records for BHS's other special collections, as well as subject research guides. Emma also enables the integration of descriptive records with digitized collection materials and other digital media, opening up many new possibilities for collection use and discovery.

In the process, 402 accessions that shared a common provenance but had been treated as separate collections were identified and brought back together into 201 individual collections, greatly easing access to these materials and increasing their research value. Taken together, these accomplishments represent a remarkable increase in access to collections compared to the five records that had been available online just four years earlier. By these standards, the staff judged the project as an overwhelming success, though some new challenges have already presented themselves in the year since its completion.[11]

Broader access to the collections has not only increased the number of library visitors and remote reference requests but has also changed the overall nature of patrons' inquiries. Whereas in the past, patrons would contact or visit BHS to ask vague questions about what materials it has on a given topic, they now more often search the collections online themselves and request appointments to use specific materials. Although in some ways this has eased the overall burden on reference staff, it has increased it in other ways and exposes some of the shortcomings of MPLP processing when coupled with greater collections access.

Time saved in mediating resource discovery is now spent answering a higher number of requests, locating specifically requested materials in collections that lack box- and folder-level inventories, and helping patrons understand how to use the new search portals and descriptive records. Further complicating matters is the fact that patrons sometimes seek information that is not provided in the minimal, collection-level records. The loss of the project staff's extensive collections knowledge at the end of the survey exacerbated this considerably.

Increased access to the collections has had quite a positive impact on BHS's primary mission as a museum and educational center by providing the wider institutional staff with knowledge of the collections that they never previously had. Whereas in the past BHS staff members relied almost entirely on the library staff as experts and gatekeepers to the collections, they are now able to do their own research easily and efficiently. Among other things, this has allowed BHS the capability to develop exhibits and educational materials on a wider array of topics than ever before, use more resources from the collections in their work, rely less on materials loaned from other institutions, and display materials that have never previously been on view.

By implementing the AT, developing clear and consistent arrangement and description practices with strong supporting documentation, compiling survey ratings data, and composing baseline descriptive records, we achieved levels of physical and intellectual control over BHS's collections that had never previously existed. Implementation of the AT, coupled with our arrangement and description manuals, forms a robust infrastructure to support accessioning, processing, description, and collection management workflows that continues to be utilized and built upon by the BHS library staff. When analyzed and combined with data about collection use, the compiled survey ratings data could be used to inform and prioritize next steps for a variety of potential projects, including more detailed arrangement and description, preservation, and further digitization.

LESSONS LEARNED

With the benefit of hindsight, we were able to see how the postproject experience for the institution might have been improved by even more holistic thinking in the planning stages. First and foremost, we would suggest starting to plan for an increase in collection use postproject, even before the project begins. The increased visibility of the collections will invariably lead to increased use, whether in person or via remote reference questions. Start planning for reallocation of staff hours, advocating for additional hours or positions, implementing a reference internship program, training volunteers, fund-raising, or whatever else you can do to be ready for increased use and the impact on your staff. In addition, having a solid program of keeping reference statistics in place before or early in the project is essential to show use patterns and use them to advocate for more help.

One of the biggest shocks to the system of BHS library staff was simply how much the staff shrank when the project was complete and those four staff positions were gone, and the loss of the deep knowledge of the collections that the survey staff had built over the course of the project. Though permanent staff did supervise the project work, they didn't have nearly the same level of day-to-day involvement with, and learning about, our collection holdings. In retrospect, we would suggest including a full-time member of your staff in a survey project if at all possible, rather than relying solely on project staff. A great deal of institutional and collection knowledge is built through the process that is a shame to lose at project end.

While we were fortunate in not having too many unexpected surprises along the way, we would still advocate for knowing as much as you can about your collections at the outset of the project. Because the BHS collections were relatively small and fit all in one storage space, our staff had spent a good amount of time dealing physically with the collections and had a solid understanding of their size and condition as a whole. But we could have fallen significantly behind in the project had we run into serious condition or preservation concerns or inaccurately estimated the size or number of collections. We would strongly suggest that institutions with larger holdings or off-site storage think carefully about what initial steps they need to take, such as an initial survey of a small sampling of collections, condition assessment sampling, or shelf reading and shelf-lists, to understand their backlog of hidden collections well enough to accurately plan a similar project.

There are a number of things we did that we feel were particularly valuable in the day-to-day implementation of the project plan. Front-loading the bigger, more complicated collections in the survey phase allowed the team to make sure that this work would be done thoroughly and honed their arrangement and description chops, making later work go by more quickly and efficiently. Similarly, our regular team meetings, especially at the outset of the project, were very important. These structured check-ins allowed for consistent supervision and for clear and informed decision making as issues arose that required defining or refining of arrangement and description practices. This ensured consistency in description work and also generally made the project staff more skilled and efficient in their work, as everyone knew the expectations and policies and felt invested in them because they had helped to shape them. It also allowed for project staff and long-term staff to transfer knowledge to the benefit of the descriptive work.

These regular meetings were particularly helpful in shaping our approach to doing collection-level descriptive work. This turned out to be among the biggest—and most interesting—challenges of our project. We needed to find a balance between being efficient and minimal enough to keep on the project timeline and our desire to provide robust and useful description. These meetings gave us a chance to reflect on and hone what MPLP meant for our institution and for this particular project. It allowed us time to discuss who our users were, how they asked questions, and what kind of information would be most valuable to provide within the confines of collection-level description. We would encourage any institution doing a large-scale MPLP project to take the time to discuss what this approach means at their institution and how they can use it to best effect the level of work they are doing.

The major change to the project plan in retrospect would be to begin the output of EAD and MARC records earlier in the project, instead of waiting until the final phase and having just one person be responsible for this work. Our fear was that tasking the full survey team with this work would take time away from surveying and processing, but in hindsight, it would have made the final phase of the project go more smoothly and freed up Matthew to do some additional, beneficial processing work on certain collections. The export process was detailed, mundane work that could have been made less burdensome had it been shared by the full team.

CONCLUSION

Looking back at the project now that it is complete, it is a model we would wholeheartedly advocate to other institutions who might find themselves in a similar situation to the one that BHS was in just four years ago. Planning a project with clear, realistic objectives and leveraging and building upon the proven, successful methods of our colleagues and peer institutions enabled us to accomplish our intended goals of gaining baseline physical and intellectual control over all of our archival collections, creating online-accessible descriptive records to increase access, and building both a descriptive and decision-making infrastructure that can be iterated upon in future work. Because we amassed as much knowledge as possible about our collections at the project's outset and approached our work in a thoughtful, flexible manner, we were able to effectively alter our original project plan in order to meet unexpected challenges and avoid extra work and frustration in the long run. Regular discussion, reflection, and critique of our work not only enabled us to work more efficiently and produce higher-quality descriptive records but also made us all better archivists in general.

Though minimal description is admittedly imperfect and can unintentionally create new kinds of work and frustration for both researchers and library staff, we still maintain that it was a necessary first step for BHS's collections and that any short-term "growing pains" the institution is currently experiencing as a result of the radically increased access to collections are a phase that will pass. As BHS considers its next round of goal setting, project planning, and grant writing, it is much better prepared to create and advocate for this work with the foundation the project created. And perhaps most importantly, a significant body of Brooklyn's rich historical record is now more accessible than it has ever been in the past, and hopefully it will only become more so in years to come.

Matthew B. Gorham *is arrangement and description rrchivist at Yale University Library's Archives and Manuscripts Department. Between January 2010 and June 2012, he was project archivist at the Brooklyn Historical Society.* ***Chela Scott Weber*** *is associate head, Tamiment Library and Robert F. Wagner*

Labor Archives, New York University. Until June 2011, she was director of library and archives at the Brooklyn Historical Society.

NOTES

1. "About the Brooklyn Historical Society," Brooklyn Historical Society, 2013, accessed June 1, 2013, www.brooklynhistory.org/about/mission.html.
2. "Brooklyn Historical Society Archives," Brooklyn Historical Society, August 25, 2007, accessed June 1, 2013, http://web.archive.org/web/20070825003135/http://www.brooklynhistory.org/library/archives.html.
3. Brooklyn Historical Society. "2007–2011 Strategic Plan," Brooklyn, N.Y., 2007.
4. Matthew Lyons, "Assessing Collections with the HSP Survey Method," *Fondly, Pennsylvania* (blog), September 22, 2011, http://hsp.org/blogs/fondly-pennsylvania/assessing-collections-with-the-hsp-survey-method.
5. Philadelphia Area Consortium of Special Collections, *PACSCL Consortial Survey Initiative Project Documentation,* April 16, 2008, accessed June 11, 2013, www.pacsclsurvey.org/documentation.html.
6. Christine Weideman, "Accessioning As Processing," *The American Archivist* 69, no. 2 (Fall/Winter 2006): 274–83.
7. Mark A. Greene and Dennis Meissner, "More Product, Less Process: Revamping Traditional Archival Processing," *The American Archivist* 68, no. 2 (Fall/Winter 2005): 208–63.
8. Robert S. Cox, "Maximal Processing, or, Archivist on a Pale Horse," *Journal of Archival Organization* 8, no. 2 (2010): 134–48.
9. Chela Scott Weber, "Metro & ACRL/NY present: Catablogging—Leveraging Blogging Software to Present Your Collections on the Web," *Vimeo,* March 10, 2012, accessed June 1, 2013, http://vimeo.com/41963924; Brooklyn Historical Society, *Emma: The Catablog of Archives, Manuscripts, and Special Collections at Brooklyn Historical Society,* accessed June 1, 2013, http://brooklynhistory.org/library/wp/.
10. Philadelphia Area Consortium of Special Collections, *Project Documentation,* 2013, accessed June 12, 2013, http://clir.pacscl.org/project-documentation/.
11. The authors are grateful to current BHS library staff members Julie May, Elizabeth Call, and Jacob Nadal for their generosity in sharing their insight regarding how the project has affected the library and the postproject realities of their work.

FOUR

Step by Step, Stage by Stage

Getting a Diverse Backlog of Legacy Finding Aids Online

Eira Tansey, Tulane University

Across the country, many archives have legacy descriptive information that is still "hidden" to most researchers. This information may take the form of finding aids found only in reading room binders, internal staff files, and unstructured web guides. According to a 2010 OCLC survey, despite decades of effort, a significant volume of archival collections still remain hidden due to the lack of online description. Surveyed respondents reported that 44 percent of archival material is not described online.[1] Although many archives have made strides in implementing EAD and migrating legacy finding aids, finding the time and resources to move this information to a modern format poses significant challenges for most archives.

The Louisiana Research Collection (LaRC) has collections with research potential for wide audiences. Preserving more than four linear miles of archival and print materials, LaRC has particular strengths in New Orleans Carnival and Mardi Gras, the Civil War, Jewish studies, LGBT studies, Louisiana politics, social welfare, and Southern literature. Prior to 2009, it had only a handful of online finding aids. We also had the same kinds of limited resources other archives face, and so while making information about our holdings more widely available was a priority, it was also an intimidating prospect. But it was one we chose to tackle head-on. This case study explores the path we took to migrate our legacy finding aids to an online format. I share my experience over the past four years leading a major project to standardize our archival description, migrate several hundred legacy finding aids to the web, and prioritize underdescribed collections for finding aid creation.

This path took different forms. Over time, the project divided naturally into three distinct phases, dictated by the different levels of description available for materials. Each of these phases used a different strategy to migrate information online. We used a combination of internal resources and vendor-provided data entry (which originated in the recovery of our collections damaged in the aftermath of Hurricane Katrina and was significantly expanded to involve legacy data migration for 500 undamaged collections). Our approach has run the gamut from "quick and dirty" to designating collections for complete rearrangement and description. As of this writing, our overall migration efforts are still ongoing, although the end of major migration activities is slowly creeping into sight.

As a result of all these projects, 70 percent of LaRC's holdings are now described online. Our holdings are more accessible to the public, and we are finding that we are reaching many new users as a result.

PLANNING

The Louisiana Research Collection (LaRC) is a research library and archives, part of the Special Collections division of Tulane University's Howard-Tilton Memorial Library. While LaRC has a significant collection of material both in scope and volume, it has a comparatively lean staffing situation. LaRC's four staff members include the head (who reports to the director of special collections), an archives catalog librarian, a public services librarian (with both reference and print acquisition duties), and a library associate for archives processing and digital initiatives (myself). My position has primary responsibility for overall archival collection management, including the creation of finding aids. LaRC is one of five special collections units but manages virtually all of its archival activities among its four dedicated staff members. Most of LaRC's archival processing tasks are handled by student workers and interns, under my supervision.

In 2008, all of our finding aids were still being created as word processing documents. They were printed out and put in binders in our reading room. A handful of finding aids existed on our website, but these were simple HTML files and not EAD encoded. Other than the handful online, the only way researchers could access our finding aids was to come to Tulane or contact us to request a copy. Although we sometimes had recent computer file versions of finding aids, the vast majority of our finding aids did not have any kind of electronic record. Shortly after I arrived, I began scanning any requested paper-based finding aids as PDFs (with optical character recognition [OCR] capabilities to support text search) and saved a copy on our shared network drive for future use.

Many of these were eventually placed on our website; however, this provided only limited functionality.

In the past, subject and collection catalog cards were created and placed in the old card catalog, which to this day is still used in our reading room (although as more goes online, it is no longer the first point of research). An archives catalog librarian came to LaRC in 2008 to perform original MARC cataloging for our collections. The cataloging librarian looked at the original archival descriptions in addition to the collections themselves to guide cataloging efforts. Our MARC cataloging only covers basic collection-level information and, until Archon was implemented in 2009, continued to direct patrons to contact staff for a copy of the finding aid. Although these collection-level MARC records began to make our holdings more accessible since they showed up in our online public access catalog (OPAC) and WorldCat, discovery of collections and their contents remained limited. Clearly a change was needed, and we started exploring ways to facilitate finding aid access over the web.

I began by taking a complete survey of our processed collections, assessing whether a finding aid existed, and if it did, how much additional work it needed to be ready to share with the public.[2] This process took several months over the course of 2009. I found that finding aids ranged in detail from large published catalogs with item-level descriptions to one-page box-level inventories. The finding aids also varied wildly in accuracy, as many had never been updated to reflect accruals.

I collected all my initial data on notepads and later logged it in Microsoft Excel. All collections were first recorded as having a finding aid or no finding aid. If a finding aid existed, the quality was then examined. This was a subjective process, but finding aids were generally classified as "in progress" for collections currently being processed, "ready to go" for collections where the finding aid was more or less free of errors and consistent with the housing of the collection, "minor work needed" if some small problems existed such as an accrual of one box not reflected in the current finding aid, or "major work needed" for finding aids that existed but required major staff revision in order to be useful.

The survey found the following results for our processed manuscript collections:

- Ready to go finding aids: 380 total, or 40 percent of our collections
- Minor work needed finding aids: 138 total, or 14.5 percent of our collections
- Major work needed finding aids: 55 total, or 6 percent of our collections
- Collections without finding aids ("nothing"): 375 total, or 39.5 percent of our collections

Between late 2008 and early 2009, two New Orleans archives began to use Archon to manage and share collections information online: the Touro

Infirmary Archives and the Amistad Research Center. The Touro Infirmary archivist demonstrated Archon at the winter 2008 meeting of the Greater New Orleans Archivists. The Amistad Research Center, which like us did not have any kind of encoded finding aids, selected Archon to migrate their finding aids online. As we considered beginning to use Archon in the summer of 2009, I met with Amistad Research Center staff member Laura Thomson, who demonstrated the software to me. I also contacted Amy Schindler of the College of William & Mary after finding their presentation slides on the "Archon Ultimatum" online.[3] William & Mary had a similar situation to ours in terms of department longevity, number of collections, varying quality of finding aids, and size of staff. William & Mary, instead of rekeying their finding aids entirely, including box and folder listings, chose to attach PDFs of inventories to basic Archon collection records. Afterward, they prioritized which finding aids warranted complete rekeying. We ultimately adopted a similar method for our initial Phase 1 implementation of Archon.

Working with Tulane's Technology Services department, we requested an instance of Archon to be set up for Special Collections. I spent the next several weeks learning how to use the system and writing basic guides for our staff and students. The Amistad Research Center provided me with a copy of their user guide, which I significantly adapted for our purposes and needs.

I began training students on how to use Archon, including complete rekeying of finding aids. At the same time, I began developing a plan for how we might get all of the "ready to go" and "minor work needed" finding aids in the system. It became clear that even with our wonderful student workers, completely rekeying the box and folder listings of each finding aid was not realistic at that point. For our first phase of legacy finding aid migration, we began to implement what we now refer to as the "quick and dirty" method. The phases we experienced over the course of this project developed as we went along. While we have always worked toward an ideal of complete archival description for all holdings, phases emerged based on resources available as the project grew.

IMPLEMENTATION

Phase 1: Quick and Dirty

Our goal for this first phase of finding aid migration was to quickly create collection-level finding aids for many of our most highly used collections. We selected a few to rekey in their entirety.

For any collections that already had MARC cataloging, we first imported the MARC record into Archon, cleaned up the data (that is, by transferring data that had been imported incorrectly to more appropriate fields), and added boilerplate language regarding access and citations. We then scanned the legacy finding aid, attached it to the Archon record, and added a note highlighting the attached legacy finding aid to the collection-level record. This enabled patron access to the scanned box and folder inventory. I trained our student workers to perform most of these steps and assigned them new collections to input each week. After they completed them, I created subject headings and creator authorities based on the MARC record, approved the collection record (that is, the finding aid) for public access, and created a staff-view-only separate accession record. Over time, the cataloging librarian updated the MARC record with links to the finding aid.

After doing this for a few months, we had input most of the MARC-cataloged collections. I then began to prioritize collections with no MARC records for Archon input. Once a collection was entered in Archon by the students with basic descriptive information from the legacy finding aid and accession documentation, and then approved and made public by me, we sent the information to our cataloging librarian. She cataloged the collection in Voyager and WorldCat with a direct link to the Archon finding aid and assigned subject headings and creator authorities, which were added to the Archon record later.

By fall 2010, we had approximately 80 basic collection-level finding aids in Archon and approximately 7 fully rekeyed (based on legacy documentation) finding aids. In addition, all finding aids for newly processed collections were being created in Archon. The migration of legacy finding aids was carried out with one staff member (me) and several student workers working 10–15 hours a week. Our cataloging librarian also performed additional authorities and subject heading work inside Archon.

Phase 2: Working with a Vendor

Phase 1 had been an excellent start to making our collections more widely available to the public. However, we still had a significant amount of catch-up in order to not only create collection-level finding aids for virtually all of our holdings but also to convert the inventories of more legacy finding aids to facilitate deeper access to collections. Our work through this point garnered significant attention and support from the library administration, and our associate dean located money to support vendor migration of several hundred finding aids.

The vendor portion of the legacy finding aid migration dovetailed with previously contracted work with collections damaged in the aftermath of Hurricane Katrina. In late 2010, we initiated a new project with the vendor that had done the recovery and restoration work on the damaged collections (now located at our off-site facility, where the vendor had set up offices). This new project would support creation of fuller finding aids for the restored collections (which then had only brief initial recovery inventories; legacy finding aids existed for some restored collections and were used where applicable, and the migration of several hundred legacy finding aids for undamaged collections in our main on-site building.

The funding for this phase was available only as a lump sum and tied directly to capitalizing on the inventory of the restored collections flooded after Katrina, although this was university funded rather than FEMA funded (as the initial inventories for the restored collections had been). With a lump-sum amount, our vendor needed to agree to a flat fee for the project as a whole, which was a significant gamble on their part, but it ultimately proved to be a successful partnership, resulting in a huge volume of standardized archival description being made available to researchers. An immediate opportunity was there to create useful finding aids from the Katrina-related restored collection inventories, as well as for our undamaged collections that had finding aids in "ready to go" or "minor work needed" condition.

The creation of finding aids for the recovery project involved creating 80 finding aids. Some of these collections were very large and the finding aids had folder-level inventories, resulting in a total descriptive volume of at least a half-million folders for the recovered collections. The restored collections typically did not have usable finding aids, so these collections warranted new finding aid creation.

The second part of the contract with the vendor covered migration of 500 legacy finding aids for high-priority undamaged collections, housed at our main building (that is, on site). These 500 were finding aids identified in my survey as being in good enough shape to rekey (down to the inventory level), requiring only what we thought would be minimal review (the "ready to go" and "minor work needed" finding aids). Many of these were finding aids that already had basic collection-level records created in Archon during Phase 1.

Preparing the legacy finding aids for delivery to the vendor was crucially important. The biggest challenge was that we were responsible for ensuring the accuracy of all the descriptions. Since all data entry was performed off-site with no physical transfers of material, the vendor had no role in verifying the contents of the descriptions. Therefore, in order to prevent "garbage in–garbage out" results, we had to review each finding aid against the physical holdings to ensure accuracy before sending it. As we began the review process for finding aids I previously thought were in pretty good shape, we found that "pretty good" was relative, as these often had typos, incorrect dates or folder titles, or even missing boxes.

We developed a multistep workflow for the legacy finding aid review process that involved myself and student workers:

1. I identified batches of legacy finding aids for review and assigned them to student workers.

2. Student workers then photocopied each finding aid to annotate, took the finding aid copy into the stacks, and:
    - Checked that all boxes and volumes listed on the finding aid were on the shelf. If there were more or less, this was noted on the finding aid. For finding aids arranged at the folder level, the finding aid was checked at that level.
    - Checked dates and/or names where needed.
    - For calendar-style finding aids (i.e., where everything is listed without box or folder notation), the student noted which boxes/folders the items were in.
    - Noted any missing folders, boxes, or volumes.
3. Student workers then turned over all annotated finding aids to me. I did a quick review to make sure they were ready for data entry and then filled out a cover sheet with any special instructions to the vendor.
4. I scanned all the annotated finding aids through our office copier/scanner to save the finding aids as PDFs. The files were renamed for usability and recorded in two places (our master spreadsheet of all LaRC collections and our list of finding aids sent to the vendor). I then sent these files (typically three to six per day over nine months) in an email to the vendor staff, copied to library administrators.
5. I then returned the physical annotated copies to a student worker, who filed them in binders containing all documentation sent to the vendor.

We provided the vendor with sets of data entry templates for Archon and in-house style guidelines (which applied to both restored collections and legacy finding aids). They were also instructed to consult *Describing Archives: A Content Standard (DACS)* for any further clarification. In addition to rekeying what we sent, the vendor created additional information if it was not in the legacy finding aid (primarily creator information and authorities, and subject/genre headings). This was intended to create standardized and consistent information and access points for all of our finding aids. Everything the vendor created was done in a staff-view-only mode, as we had a process for reviewing all work before public release. The information the vendor was responsible for rekeying, modifying, or creating (if necessary) included collection-level information (including scope), creator information and authorities, subject and genre headings, and inventories.

The process for reviewing the vendor's work took up a significant amount of my time. The workflow to release the vendor's finding aids consisted of the following steps (this workflow applied primarily to the migrated legacy finding aids):

1. If the vendor had any questions about finding aids we transmitted, they asked them at our weekly meetings at their site. I then looked into these questions over the course of the week and emailed them the answers.
2. The vendor periodically sent us an email noting which finding aids had been created and were ready for our review and public release (the finished finding aids were set to staff-view only at the point of vendor handoff back to me). Each email included an updated spreadsheet with a master list of finding aids they had finished.
3. As part of my review and public release process, I first created a basic staff-view-only Archon accession file record (which contains confidential information about how we acquired the collection and whether a deed of gift exists, any donor relations notes, etc.). Then I checked the vendor-created Archon finding aid. I briefly made sure that the inventory matched what the marked-up finding aid stated (e.g., if we sent them a finding aid that showed eight boxes and five volumes, I quickly checked to make sure the Archon finding aid showed the same). If there were any major revisions needed, I informed the vendor and did not release it.
4. If everything on the Archon finding aid looked accurate, I made the finding aid available to the public (i.e., taking it out of staff-view only) and updated all relevant internal documentation.
5. I periodically sent updates on the new finding aid releases to the LaRC archives catalog librarian.
6. The archives catalog librarian then created new MARC records for the collections with migrated finding aids (or updated previously created MARC records), including adding a link to the Archon finding aid. As she was doing so, she informed me of any further typos or discrepancies she saw in the finding aid that were not caught earlier. If they were minor, I changed them. If they were major, then we informed the vendor to make the changes.

We eventually ended up sending 511 legacy finding aids to the vendor for migration. Although we completed the legacy portion of the project much more quickly than originally anticipated, reviewing, manually correcting, and transferring these finding aids to the vendor took us nine months (from January to September of 2011), and fulfilling our responsibilities for the contract occupied me and my students for the better part of that year. All legacy finding aids covered under this contract were released by June 2012, with the majority made public by the end of 2011. The vendor also finished creating finding aids for the Katrina-recovered collections in early 2012.

Phase 3: Dealing with Odds and Ends

Phases 1 and 2 only dealt with major collections that already had some kind of legacy finding aid in manageable condition (classified as "ready to go" and "minor work needed" in my initial survey). These phases did not cover collections without finding aids or those with finding aids that needed major work, and they also did not include any work associated with our other smaller collection classes. These other collections are known as the M- and B-collections. They are typically smaller in scope and size than the "regular" collections but contain significant holdings that often fly under the radar of both staff and users.

Regarding the major collections without finding aids (or that have legacy finding aids so unruly that they essentially need to be re-created), we are currently prioritizing those that most closely fit our current collection development policy and for which we anticipate the highest use. Since many of these collections often require some reprocessing, we typically assign these to campus interns. LaRC is a campus partner with Tulane University's Center for Public Service (CPS), which directs students from diverse majors to public service internship opportunities. (Tulane University requires undergraduate students to perform public service activities for graduation.) CPS interns work with us for one semester and need a finished project they can point to as a product of their internship. We have found that having CPS interns work on reprocessing and/or rewriting the finding aids for these particular collections has been extremely successful. We often identify CPS interns' strengths when matching them with a collection. For example, French-language majors have written deeper and more useful finding aids for our French-language holdings. We will likely handle the B-collections (which consist solely of bound materials such as scrapbooks) in a similar fashion once we have made more progress in other migration areas.

Beginning in fall 2012, we took major strides to create finding aids for the more than 1,150 M-collections. The M-collections are very small collections of one to two folders, often containing only a diary or a few letters. Despite the seemingly modest nature of the M-collections, they contain significant holdings in high demand by users, such as letters written by notable Civil War figures, diaries kept by a diverse group of New Orleanians, slave documents, political photographs, and so on. Virtually all of the M-collections have very simple single-form accession records, accessible only to staff. We retooled our student worker workflow from Phase 1 to support rapid entry of this information. The workflow consisted of:

1. Comparing the original accession form to the actual M-collection.
2. Creating a new accession record in Archon based on the information from the original accession form.

3. Creating a collection record in Archon based on the information from the original accession form and the materials themselves, if necessary.
4. Documenting (in a spreadsheet) progress through the M-collections.
5. Review and approval of the Archon collection and accession records by me, making any necessary changes. The collection record is then made available to the public and sent on to the catalog librarian for MARC record creation.

One of the major differences between this workflow and previous phases is that students handled the creation of Archon accession records. We made this change because M-collections were typically acquired in very simple circumstances that did not require reviewing sensitive donor relations documents, and the necessary information was usually listed in the accession form. Transferring the responsibility for creating Archon-based accession records to the students relieved a major burden from me.

LaRC has always been fortunate to have incredible student workers, and two of them were able to enter approximately 1,100 M-collections over the course of two semesters (Fall 2012 and Spring 2013). Our student workers generally work between 8 and 12 hours a week, and balance work projects between paging and reshelving duties. We anticipate completion and release of all the M-collections will be accomplished within the next year (2014).

RESULTS

In our view, our efforts at large-scale finding aid migration have been an unqualified success. Our finding aids are now created according to a common set of standards, reflecting DACS and consistent in-house practices. We've gone from having only a couple of online finding aids available in 2008 to creating online finding aids for 70 percent of our collections by mid-2013. These finding aids are often within the first few Google search results and so have connected us to many new users and potential users who have never been exposed to archives before. We have tracked Archon use in Google Analytics since early 2013, and approximately 44 percent of Archon traffic comes from search engines (85 percent coming from Google searches). In addition to the finding aids available through our own website, we have contributed EAD files generated from the Archon records to ArchiveGrid, OCLC's international archival finding aid database. Our archives catalog librarian continues to create MARC records for our collections, ensuring that those who start their search via WorldCat or Tulane's library catalog will continue to discover our holdings and have access to our finding aids through links to Archon.

An interesting result of getting so many finding aids online has been the exposure of collections that were previously underused. Even before our finding aids went online, many researchers knew about our "greatest hits" collections—collections we were known for, that had been frequently cited, and that had published catalogs. After putting finding aids online for the "long tail" of our collections (in addition to the "greatest hits"), it has been exciting to see many of these collections accessed for the first time.[4]

Since September 2008, we have tracked use of collections by noting how many patrons request a given collection per month. We've noted that many of the collections that were not well known previous to migration were used for the first time following the public release of the finding aid. We've found that over 140 collections were requested for the first time (since September 2008) following finding aid release. While there is not necessarily a direct connection between putting the finding aid online and the first pull, it seems likely that the greater exposure increases interest in collections and exposes more sources than just those cited in previous works or our "greatest hits."

This pattern fits in with a growing trend of increased use of our department's resources. The Louisiana Research Collection has experienced significant growth in use over the past five years. Between 2009 and 2012, we have experienced a 37-percent increase in reading room use. Some of this is likely attributable to the increased availability of online finding aids, in addition to improved reference services and expanded outreach and instruction.

One of the often overlooked but critical benefits of getting our finding aids online was that learning about our collections is no longer a physically bound activity. In the past, researchers would often spend a full day in the reading room browsing the finding aid binders just to prepare for their research. Now, many of them walk in with a long list of what they plan to view during their visit. In a time when travel money is scarce and researchers need to maximize their time in the reading room, this has been a significant improvement to the researcher experience.

Standardizing and having online access to archival description has also had significant benefits for LaRC staff. It has greatly aided our ability to perform reference duties, compile information on specific holdings, and manage our overall collections.

In addition to freeing the finding aids from the restrictions of the reading room, there is another benefit: If a disaster visited our building, we'd no longer lose all of the documentation related to our collections. While many of LaRC's collections were severely damaged in the aftermath of flooding associated with Hurricane Katrina, we were lucky that our documentation survived intact. Now, our finding aids and supplementary accession records within Archon are backed up consistently on a university server, which has off-site backup capabilities. Getting the finding aids online was as much a strategy for emergency preparedness as an effort for increased collections accessibility.

LESSONS LEARNED

One of the major lessons we learned from our experience was that before beginning any sort of finding aid migration project, archivists should ruthlessly determine what should be migrated. Migration is a time- and labor-intensive process, even if it's outsourced. The first step should be to identify finding aids that shouldn't be candidates for migration at all, such as those in which the description and inventory clearly does not match the reality of what's in the collection (as we did). Those finding aids will likely have to be rewritten or the collection reprocessed. Although it wasn't part of our analysis, you may also want to consider whether collections might be possible candidates for deaccessioning as part of this process. Finding aid migration might not make sense for these collections.

After identifying what to migrate, it is important to prioritize what to migrate first and what to migrate later on. This step is critically important if there is limited money and staff to devote to migration activities. Factors to consider in deciding what to migrate initially should include:

- Quality of the finding aid (e.g., ones that can be entered as-is and accurately reflect the reality of the contents)
- How frequently collections are used
- Potential for increased research demand if more people know about the collection
- Potential impact on donor relations by making the finding aid available online

Once the universe of finding aids has been prioritized, be prepared to review every finding aid against the collection before migration. The findings may be surprising.

During our initial finding aid survey, we found that some of them had a strange narrative approach to an inventory, which we referred to as a "choose your own adventure" version of description. Clearly these would need quite a bit of revision and were not good candidates for migration. Even finding aids we thought were in excellent shape turned out to have problems preventing easy migration. If I were redesigning the initial survey knowing what I know now, I would have incorporated a greater degree of reconciliation against the physical contents of the collection (something that we did not do comprehensively until we obtained money to go forward with vendor-based migration).

During the multiple phases of migration, we have had to constantly reassess project timelines for completion. This perhaps shouldn't have come as a surprise, since we had few precedents to guide our efforts. Our progress has not always been smooth and was frequently interrupted by other priorities. Fortunately, except for the vendor-based contract, we've been able to take as much time as we needed to work through the phases. However, as we've had to frequently change workflows and projected timelines, managing user expectations has been critical. As we delivered more and more finding aids online, we have had to communicate with users that there are still gaps between available online description and what we have in our holdings.

However, the area in which we've learned the most lessons has been from our work on Phase 2, when we used the services of a library vendor for migrating legacy finding aids. Working with a vendor brings on many unique challenges, particularly because contract terms may limit flexibility or workflow changes. (See textbox 4.1 for specific points to consider in working with a vendor.)

We experienced significant benefits from working with a vendor. Because of their staffing, they can often bring more labor to the endeavor than many repositories can muster (as was certainly the case for us), and in theory, these should be qualified staff. In addition, having an extra set of eyes going over the finding aid meant they often caught things that we did not. (However, I am not sure this is a function of the vendor's role as it is simply the advisability of having multiple people reviewing legacy finding aids.)

On the other hand, when a vendor's work is performed off-site, as ours was, there can be major challenges in ensuring the efficiency and accuracy of any work being performed. This is particularly true if you're working with a vendor in which no physical temporary transfer of material is taking place. This not only forced us to devote significant labor to the project—indeed, more than we had anticipated—because we needed to verify the accuracy of the finding aids against the materials but also made minor problems more difficult. Discrepancies or gaps in the data and clarifying information necessary to establish authorities and subject headings were discussed during weekly meetings at the vendor's off-site location, not on-site where the materials could be physically checked. This required significant investigation and follow-up from me after every weekly meeting.

Overall we had very few problems with simple data entry considering the massive amount of migration that occurred, but there were often challenges establishing subject headings and creator authorities for the legacy finding aids. This was possibly due to the incomplete and inconsistent nature of the legacy archival description and again required follow-up on my part to provide or correct information.

Clearly, there can be both considerable benefits and drawbacks to using the services of a vendor for finding aid migration. Significant staff time will still have to be expended to ensure a successful conversion.

• Determine a budget, priorities, and desired outcomes. Identify the staff member responsibility for various aspects of the project.
• Work with a vendor that has experience in working with archival projects. Many vendors have significant library experience, but it's important that they understand the particular description needs and best practices associated with archival holdings.
• Contracts should stipulate the archival functions to be completed, and be as detailed as realistically possible. When we were creating the contract in 2010, it was reviewed by several levels of staff members, including myself. This created a strong and comprehensive contract, since various stakeholders brought their expertise to its creation.
• Stipulate in the contract how errors in data entry should be handled. Specify a time limit for how long the vendor should be responsible for correcting mistakes, because there may be some significant time between when the vendor migrates the finding aid, and when you get a chance to review the work.
• Require that the vendor use well-established resources, such as EAD, DACS, and Library of Congress Authorities, and provide tutorials or guidelines for in-house metadata practices where applicable.
• Do not just hand off the project and come back later; have periodic check-ins, with significant review at the beginning in order to gauge the quality of the work and adjust expectations. The amount of overview could take up much more time than you anticipate, but it is crucial for ensuring that resources are well-spent.
• Assess your own situation and determine whether a vendor is the best solution for your institution's needs. In some cases, a vendor might be the only realistic solution. For smaller or less complex projects, well-supervised paid internships for archival studies students might be appropriate. The criteria involved in such a decision should revolve around the quantity and quality of archival description to be migrated.

Textbox 4.1. Specific points to consider when working with a vendor on finding aid migration.

Using a vendor is not a one-size-fits-all solution, and each archive must evaluate the quality and quantity of the legacy finding aids to be converted, as well as consider both the extent and limitations of its resources. Outsourcing is not a panacea, and one must consider how much staff time will still be required to oversee the vendor's work. Careful planning at the outset and ongoing monitoring are the keys to a successful vendor relationship.

CONCLUSION

In the past four years at the Louisiana Research Collection, we've successfully overcome the significant challenges posed by migrating our legacy archival descriptions. While the three phases of this project were not completely envisioned at the beginning, we were able to develop them iteratively based on the progress we made and the flexibility we embraced in developing migration strategies. During each phase we tried to make the best use of the resources we had available. While at times the workload seemed overwhelming, we had a strong institutional commitment to making our collections more accessible to all users. When I was developing my initial spreadsheet of the state of our finding aids, it seemed impossible to believe that we could ever make any kind of rapid progress in getting them online.

As of this writing, 70 percent of our holdings have some form of online description. We are not yet done, but the end of major migration is in sight, and we now have workflows and documentation in place to support the final stretch. The proliferation of online finding aids has coincided with a significant increase in reference queries and reading room use by patrons. It has made the work of LaRC staff more efficient. It has allowed us to be able to contribute our finding aids to major portals such as ArchiveGrid, allowing us to reach even more potential users. By placing so much information about our holdings online, LaRC has made significant strides in expanding access to our holdings, reaching new users, and making the research experience more productive.

***Eira Tansey** is the digital archivist/records manager at the University of Cincinnati. Until November 2013, she was a library associate at Tulane University.*

NOTES

1. Jackie M. Dooley and Katherine Luce, *Taking Our Pulse: The OCLC Research Survey of Special Collections and Archives* (Dublin, Ohio: OCLC Research, 2010), 46, www.oclc.org/research/publications/library/2010/2010-11.pdf.

2. This survey only covered the accessioned and processed "regular" manuscripts collection. It did not apply to M- or B-collections. The M-collections are typically very small collections of one or two folders. The B-collections consist solely of bound materials such as scrapbooks. The survey also did not look at any of the off-site collections undergoing Hurricane Katrina aftermath recovery work.

3. Ute Schechter, "The ARCHON Ultimatum at the SCRC/Swem Library," presentation at the Mid-Atlantic Regional Archives Conference, Charleston, West Virginia, April 17, 2009, www.slideshare.net/SwemSCRC/the-archon-ultimatum-at-the-special-collections-research-center-swem-library and www.slideshare.net/SwemSCRC/the-archon-ultimatum-at-the-special-collections-research-center-swem-library-1321938.

4. Jane Stevenson, "The Long Tail of Archives," *Archives Hub* (blog), April 10, 2011, http://archiveshub.ac.uk/blog/2011/04/the-long-tail-of-archives/.

FIVE

You Got Your Archives in My Cataloging

A Collaborative Standards-Based Approach to Creating Item-Level Metadata for Digitized Archival Materials

Kelcy Shepherd and Kate Gerrity, Amherst College

When the Amherst College Library created a new Digital Programs department in 2011, it provided an opportunity for the library to rethink all aspects of its digital collections and the workflow that supports them. Digitization of unique and rare materials—previously inaccessible to those outside of the archives—was one of three major goals for the library, and the focus had been on just that: digitization. Digital objects without metadata, however, cannot be found and used by the researchers for whom we digitize. The need to create rich, well-structured, standards-based metadata to support discovery and understanding of digitized materials might have proven a challenge for the library's fledgling digitization program. Instead, it became an opportunity for collaboration among the Archives and Special Collections, Technical Services, and Digital Programs departments.

The creation of the new Digital Programs department to scale-up digitization was one of many changes at the library; the librarian of the college, the head of Archives and Special Collections, and the head of Digital Programs were among many new hires. It was the librarian of the college who established digitization as one of the three main goals for the library, and two of these goals—digitization and an emphasis on instruction—had a significant impact on the archives. The heavy increase in instruction, and therefore reference, had stretched the department to capacity, and there were no additional positions to support the creation of metadata for digitized archival materials. Fortunately, as a small organization (just under 42 full-time employees), the Amherst College Library lends itself to close collaboration, and we approached this as an opportunity to take advantage of and build on skill sets across departments. Since metadata creation is the evolution of cataloging for digital information, those in Technical Services, Digital Programs, and Archives and Special Collections agreed that metadata support for all digital materials, including digitized materials from the archives, would ideally be situated in the Cataloging Section, though the approach would be collaborative. Cataloging librarian Kate Gerrity had experience and training in non-MARC metadata formats, and changes in procedures and workflows had created efficiencies that allowed her to devote more time to the new metadata program, so shifting responsibility for this work was a logical choice.

The head of Digital Programs, Kelcy Shepherd, worked closely with Kate to develop, test, and refine procedures for creating rich, granular, structured metadata for digitized archival materials. Kelcy's eight years working as an archivist had focused on various aspects of description and descriptive standards, including teaching the Describing Archives: A Content Standard (DACS) workshop for the Society of American Archivists. Given this background, Kelcy became the primary archival voice in the process, with additional input from the archives. Kate was given an orientation to Archives and Special Collections and participated in DACS training to help provide background in archival principles and archival description. In addition, our first project drew upon existing metadata created in the archives, paving the way for her transition into archival description. While developing knowledge of archival practices beyond the archives itself was necessary to the success of our metadata practices, we also recognized that scaling up the creation of digital collections, enabling more effective discovery by users, and developing metadata that could be readily shared would require an approach that would integrate the principles of archival description with best practices from the broader metadata and digital library communities.

This case study describes the development of best practices and workflow for the creation of item-level metadata for digitized archival materials at the Amherst College Library. It discusses the selection of content standards, vocabularies, and a schema for archival digital objects and the development of documentation, tools, and workflows to support metadata creation. We consider the challenges that arose during the process and the lessons learned along the way. We explore the aspects that make our collaboration effective, particularly the integration of two sometimes divergent perspectives: the archivist and the cataloger. Finally, we consider the outcomes of our work and plans for the future.

PLANNING

Developing a new methodology for creating metadata for digitized archival materials was part of a larger formal plan for the newly created Digital Programs department to establish a more programmatic approach to building digital collections. This initial two-year plan (2011–2013), written in consultation with the other departments involved, stated that the department would collaborate with Technical Services on metadata creation, management, and repurposing as well as establishing best practices for metadata, and with Archives and Special Collections on identifying and prioritizing collections for digitization and digital preservation, among other things. In reality, the roles of each department in the development of digital collections are not so clearly delineated. The three departments work together organically with extensive consultation and information sharing from project selection through digitization, metadata creation, establishing/refining interface requirements, and promotion.

One of the goals identified in the Digital Programs department's two-year plan was to select and use robust metadata schemas. An unstated goal was to adopt appropriate content standards and controlled vocabularies and to create rich metadata that would help users find and interpret digitized archival materials. One of the first decisions to be made was at what level to present the materials, as this would also dictate the level of description for them. Many institutions had begun exploring ways to present digitized materials without requiring item-level description. Creating a digital object for each folder, linked through minimal metadata in the container list of a finding aid, is one example. For a variety of reasons, we decided instead to create item-level descriptions for our early digital collections. The collections we digitized first were highly significant to the college or, as with Emily Dickinson's papers, to scholars at large. For many of these materials, some item-level metadata already existed and could be easily repurposed. In addition, our goals for these digital collections argue for rich, granular metadata. First, we want to share our collections and metadata as broadly as possible (through the Open Archives Initiative Protocol for Metadata Harvesting [OAI-PMH] and as Linked Open Data, for example) and feel that this can best be done with item-level metadata.[1] We also plan to create advanced chronological, geographical, and concept-mapping interfaces that will take advantage of this rich item-level metadata to allow users to analyze collections in new ways. We are in the early phases of building our digital collections, however, and we continue to revisit this decision as we scale up our digitization operations and begin to analyze the needs of various collections and of our users.

Once we decided to describe our initial digital collections at the item level, selecting a metadata schema was straightforward. Metadata Object Description Schema (MODS) had become a kind of lingua franca for many digital libraries.[2] Its roots in MARC made it feel like a natural choice given our integration of metadata creation into Technical Services. It provided a more granular structure than Dublin Core, which would make repurposing data easier in the future. And, those involved had a high comfort level with XML, the markup language used for MODS. Because we knew even during our planning stage that the ability to share our metadata outside of our own systems would be crucial to promoting our collections in the future, we also consulted the Digital Library Federation/Aquifer Implementation Guidelines for Shareable MODS Records to inform our decisions.[3]

Identifying an appropriate content standard was a little more complicated. Given Kelcy's background, our first instinct was to look to DACS. While the principles laid out in DACS apply to item-level description, Version 1.0 of the standard provides few, if any, examples for items. Because it is standard practice for archivists to describe aggregates of materials, the rules primarily approach description from that perspective, and refer to other, media-specific standards for more granular levels of description.[4] Even so, we used the DACS Optimum Requirements for Single-Level Descriptions as the basis for our own requirements for metadata records, and we continue to consult DACS as a starting point when new questions arise.[5]

To supplement DACS, we turned to Descriptive Cataloging of Rare Materials (Manuscripts) [DCRM(MSS)], still in draft.[6] Although it is not finalized, the new standard seemed far enough along in its development that we were comfortable using the existing draft. We felt that this also paved the way for us to use Descriptive Cataloging of Rare Materials (Graphics) [DCRM(G)] in the future for projects involving graphic materials such as photographs.[7] We chose to use Library of Congress Authorities as the controlled vocabulary for names and for subject headings and the Getty Art & Architecture Thesaurus, and to a lesser extent the Library of Congress Thesaurus for Graphic Materials, for genre terms.

As these efforts ramped up, the library was also collaborating with the college's Information Technology department on the selection and implementation of a new digital asset management system, which would become known as Amherst College Digital Collections (ACDC).[8] A request from our programmer for a few sample records became the impetus for our initial effort to put our decisions into practice. We first shared these records with the head of Archives and Special Collections, Mike Kelly, for input. While we had been in communication with him throughout the process, this was his first opportunity to see our work in concrete form.

Mike identified information missing from the records that would be necessary for archivists at the reference desk to retrieve materials, developed some boilerplate rights language for various scenarios, and provided overall feedback that drew upon his knowledge of the archives' researchers. For example, for items where the creator is an Amherst College alumnus, he requested that we construct an additional access point in the following form: Amherst College. Class of [YEAR]. [SURNAME]. This follows a long-standing practice for bibliographic records added to the library catalog, which was established as a result of the archives' understanding that users want to be able to search for works of alumni by class year. With this small pilot complete, we began to implement our metadata program in earnest.

IMPLEMENTATION

With the planning done and decisions and procedures in place, we started creating metadata records for two previously digitized collections: the Emily Dickinson Collection, which consists of the 850 Dickinson manuscripts held by the archives, and the Classroom Charts Collection, a collection of 61 large-format scientific drawings on cloth primarily by Orra White Hitchcock. Orra was the wife of Edward Hitchcock, the third president of Amherst College and eminent 19th-century geologist, perhaps best known for his work with fossil footprints later identified as having been formed by dinosaurs. Orra created the drawings to illustrate Edward's classroom lectures on geology and mineralogy while he was a professor at Amherst College.

Before beginning each of these projects Mike, Kate, Kelcy, and our metadata intern Adam Zukowski met to discuss the scope and nature of the collection, the presence or absence of existing metadata, and any known significant user groups. Some collection-specific decisions were made as a result of these discussions regarding such things as particular access points to add or information to be included in (or excluded from) abstracts. For example, Dickinson scholars often identify her poems by one of the two numbering systems assigned by Ralph Franklin and Thomas Johnson, so it was essential to include both numbers in addition to the manuscript numbers assigned by the archives, so that users can retrieve items by searching for these identifiers in ACDC.

To create the metadata records, we used the oXygen XML editor with a template containing our required MODS data elements. In determining which elements to require, we were committed to adhering to standards and best practices as well as making sure our metadata would be as useful and reusable as possible. Specifically, our required element set meets the standards for the DACS single-level optimum description and the Digital Library Federal (DLF)/Aquifer requirements for shareable MODS records. We diverged from the DACS optimum requirements only by not including an Administrative/Biographical History element, which we felt was unnecessary at the item level. We did, however, choose to require whenever possible an abstract, as a shortened form of Scope and Content Note. While the DLF Guidelines recommend, rather than require, the inclusion of an abstract, we felt it important to provide additional descriptive information about an object, thereby increasing its "discoverability" through a keyword search. Taken together with a link to the collection's finding aid, the abstract provides the researcher with valuable descriptive and contextual information about the object, enabling her or him to quickly evaluate its potential usefulness.

We did add a few elements to those required by DACS and the DLF Guidelines: the box and folder number in which the item is stored, and identification of the collection to which the object belongs (see figure 5.1). The box and folder number helps archivists pull materials for researchers. The link to the collection, captured in a MODS <relatedItem> element, helps to maintain the provenance of the object by linking to the finding aid for the collection. Conversely, our EAD finding aids will eventually include <dao> elements linking to the digitized items as well, though we are hoping to automate that process and have yet to implement it.

Circumstances particular to the two projects meant we were able to move through the records fairly quickly, which gave us a less-than-accurate sense of the time required to create the kind of rich item-level descriptions of archival materials our plan called for. Specifically, both collections had some existing item-level metadata that could be repurposed. Data for the Classroom Charts was in Microsoft Word format and had to be rekeyed into our MODS records, but because little was known about them we could use the same general abstract and creation date range for each record. Metadata for the Dickinson collection was in an Excel spreadsheet that we could export as XML and convert to MODS through an XSLT stylesheet. During this batch process, we were also able to popu-

Creator	Schneider, Benjamin, 1807-1877
Recipient	Hitchcock, Edward, 1793-1864
Title	Benjamin Schneider letter to Edward Hitchcock, 1848 November 20
Date	November 20, 1848
Physical Description	1 item (6 pages)
Languages	English
Place of Creation	Izmir (Turkey)
Abstract	A letter from missionary Benjamin Schneider, written upon his return from a visit to northern Syria, while performing a quarantine in Smyrna, Turkey. He writes extensively about the "Aleppo button," a skin disease that plagues the inhabitants of many towns on the banks of the Euphrates. Schneider tells Hitchcock he is sending a box with both mineral and water samples for Hitchcock to test, in an attempt to identify the cause of the disease. Schneider also writes about his mission and the happiness he feels as a result of seeing an increase in his congregation in Aintab, Syria.
Note	The header indicates the letter was written in Smyrna, the historic name for Izmir, Turkey
Genre	Correspondence
Subject	Hitchcock, Edward, 1793-1864 -- Correspondence
Subject	Leishmaniasis, Cutaneous
Subject	Turkey -- Description and travel
Subject	Missionaries -- Turkey
Subject	Reformed Church in the United States -- Missions -- Turkey
Access and Use	Public Domain: This material has been identified as being free of known restrictions under copyright law, including all related and neighboring rights. While Amherst College Archives & Special Collections claims no rights or authority over this material, we do ask that any publication or use of this material cite the Archives & Special Collections at Amherst College as the source of the images and the repository where the original documents can be found.
Part of	Edward and Orra White Hitchcock Papers
Repository	Amherst College Archives & Special Collections
Shelf Location	Box 3 Folder 36

Figure 5.1. Example metadata record showing required elements.

late the genre and some of the subject elements with preselected values, based on whether a poem or a letter was being described. Peculiarities of the Dickinson collection meant that we could not use the Date or Abstract elements in our records. Dickinson didn't date most of her manuscripts and scholars disagree about when many of the poems and letters were written. The investigation necessary to try to obtain accurate information would be enormously time consuming (and indeed often impossible since even Dickinson scholars cannot reach a consensus), so based on conversations with Mike we decided not to provide dates. We also felt we couldn't create abstracts because all of the letters are extremely brief and, well, how would you abstract a poem? While this went against our commitment to adhere to DACS and the DLF Guidelines, it contributed to faster record creation.

Several months later, we began creating MODS records for what we came to refer to as our prototype project: the Edward and Orra White Hitchcock Papers. This project typifies the kind of archival collection that is likely to be the standard fare of future digitization projects: a large archival collection with a wide range of content, in this case including correspondence, legal documents, sermons, and images, among other materials. This collection allowed us to put to the test our standards, tools, and workflows for creating metadata records from scratch for newly digitized items without any existing metadata aside from the collection's finding aid. It was with this project that we fully realized just how time consuming it is to create item-level descriptions of archival materials while adhering to best practices and standards. Though we were aware that in most cases digitization would outpace metadata creation and that we would have to make efforts to address this, the full extent of the disparity became clear with this collection. A highly unscientific sampling showed that in a single month we digitized three times as many objects as we were able to create metadata records for. While description of photographs tends to go more quickly than descriptions of manuscripts, it is still a daunting figure.

Kate and Adam, with their combined extensive background in the MARC format (from which MODS is derived), strong familiarity with non-MARC metadata, and recent graduate education experience, were quickly able to gain proficiency in the use of MODS. Some additional self-training was needed to get up to speed with DACS, which provided the archival perspective, and DCRM(MSS), which filled in the gaps left by DACS for item-level description. We also consulted DCRM(G) for materials whose graphical nature called for specialized description not accommodated by either of the other content standards.

For those three initial projects, Adam worked 20 hours per week with the amount of time devoted to metadata creation varying from week to week depending on his project workload. Initially, Kate balanced metadata creation with other job responsibilities in the Cataloging Section but has spent an increasing amount of time on work related to building the metadata program in support of Digital Programs. While she still creates metadata records, she now spends more time on review and quality control of records, training interns and staff to do metadata creation, and on workflow management along with continued exploration of best practices and investigation of tools to improve workflows and increase efficiency in metadata creation. For example, metadata creators originally kept an authority file in the form of an Excel spreadsheet but have begun to make use of the recently implemented Archivists' Toolkit to create name authority records for all names used as access points in our MODS records. Archives and Special Collections staff will benefit from the authority work done by metadata creators and metadata creators will benefit by having access to additional data within the Toolkit that could inform their description work. The Toolkit also allows the archives staff to record a range of information that does not end up in finding aids but is potentially helpful for metadata creators, particularly when trying to understand the content they are describing. The Toolkit may also help us streamline the task of embedding links to our digitized objects into the archives' encoded finding aids.

Our first metadata intern, Adam, has moved on to a full-time professional position and has been replaced with another metadata resident who splits her 35 hours a week between metadata creation and other activities that support Digital Programs. We have had two metadata interns since January 2012, both of whom quickly became proficient in deciphering 19th-century handwriting, using MODS, and applying the descriptive standards and controlled vocabularies required to create rich and accurate descriptive metadata. Recently, a staff member in the Technical Services department with a background in copy-cataloging, familiarity with XML, and an interest in history has begun training in metadata creation. While proving very promising, this trial has also highlighted the need for a modified training program for staff whose backgrounds and skill sets differ from those of graduate students in an MLIS program. Additionally, even with skilled and attentive metadata creators and clear, detailed documentation, there is always some room for interpretation when creating metadata, which means that ongoing close oversight is needed to ensure consistency as the number of metadata records we create steadily grows.

RESULTS

Our metadata efforts have been well received by staff at the archives and the library, as well as by their users. Digitized images had previously been stored in a network directory, accessible only by navigating the directory structure and interpreting file names, so archives staff can now search for and find digitized materials much more easily. Because users can also find the images without mediation, the department has less photocopying and on-demand digitization to do. This has made a particular impact with the Emily Dickinson collection, as researchers worldwide can now be directed to the digital collection.

ACDC is in the early stages of development and currently lacks the capability to generate use statistics, but this is a function for which we have advocated strongly and one that will be added soon. Knowing how much and what kind of use our collections are getting will be crucial to our ability to advocate for resources to create rich metadata for these collections and will help us form decisions on what to digitize. Although we have yet to collect user analytics or do formal assessment, we have received positive feedback from users of the digital collections. A faculty member who teaches a seminar that draws heavily on the Emily Dickinson collection immediately transitioned from her previous practice of using Thomas H. Johnson's *The Poems of Emily Dickinson* as an index to the materials to searching known items and discovering new ones in ACDC.[9] This transition did not happen with the previous digital asset management system, which also provided access to the Dickinson materials but included minimal metadata.

The librarian of the college's measure of success is how well we are supporting and enabling universal access to this content. To help meet these goals, we are promoting use of the digital collections in a number of ways. We are putting as few restrictions on the reuse of our collections as possible, and in our metadata we are making it clear to users what their rights are in regard to using our digital objects. As a result, sites such as the Dickinson Electronic Archives can make use of our freely available images.[10] Archives staff promote the collections by featuring digital content in "The Consecrated Eminence," the Archives and Special Collections' blog.[11] Mike will also be highlighting the Emily Dickinson digital collection in a forthcoming "Curator's Choice" post in the *Public Domain Review*, which focuses on open digital collections.[12]

We can further promote access and encourage use by sharing our metadata as broadly as possible, and good, structured metadata can be repurposed so that it can be pushed to a global audience in a variety of ways. By the end of 2013, we expect to be exposing our metadata through OAI-PMH, which will allow us to share our digital collections with systems such as the library's discovery tool and regional and international aggregators such as Massachusetts' Digital Commonwealth[13] and OCLC's OAIster.[14] We have mapped our metadata to schema.org in our HTML displays so that search engines can more easily understand it and integrate it into meaningful search results.[15] We are also in the process of publishing our metadata as linked open data. By increasing the ways users can discover our digital archival collections, we are supporting the library's goal of contributing to an open, global digital library.

LESSONS LEARNED

All involved in the effort are pleased with the product of our collaboration, but we can also reflect on our experience and identify areas to improve as the program evolves. Among the lessons learned, we cannot overstate the value of documentation, as obvious as it might seem. We currently have multiple sets of documentation that serve several purposes. Our general ACDC MODS Guidelines that adhere to the DLF Guidelines are essentially an application profile that incorporates instruction on the use of content standards, controlled vocabularies, and local practices on an element-by-element basis (see figure 5.2).[16] The goal is to simplify things for our metadata creators given their varying levels of experience with the standards and tools we are using, and minimize the number of sources they have to refer to when questions arise while creating metadata for digital objects. In addition, our graduate student interns have created documentation for each major collection that includes collection-specific decisions. This documentation serves as a good record of the collaborative decisions that were made (at meetings, via email, or through chance encounters in the stairwell) as issues were encountered.

This venture would not have succeeded without extensive collaboration at various levels, and not surprisingly, effective collaboration has required good communication. Communication is continual and happens both formally and informally, in scheduled and impromptu meetings, and via email. As we have ramped up digitization, the importance of good communication along with streamlined workflows has become even more apparent. With several student workers and interns digitizing and a resident and staff member creating metadata, coordination of all the parts could be a full-time job. We have found that scheduling regular meetings between those digitizing archival materials and those creating metadata is crucial to staying on top of projects and ensuring that issues are identified and addressed in a timely way so that work is not stalled. We are currently exploring project management tools that we hope will facilitate the tracking of multiple simultaneous projects at various stages of completion.

Related to the issue of communication was our discovery of the importance of relying on staff in archives to provide background and information that the metadata creators would have otherwise had to research in order to create our descriptions. This approach differs from what is common for catalogers working in a small department without subject specialists. Creating bibliographic records from scratch—that is, original cataloging—requires knowledge of both content and description, and often involves a crash course in an esoteric topic. In cataloging archival materials at the item level, Kate had to recognize that it was not necessary—or even desirable—to develop expert knowledge of the content that was being described and that it was acceptable and far more efficient

<genre>

MODS Element	Sub-elements
<genre>	None

A term that designates a category characterizing a particular style, form, or content, such as artistic, musical, literary, etc. <genre> contains terms that give more specificity than the broad terms used in <typeOfResource>. This element is repeatable.

<u>Attributes</u>

authority Use this attribute to indicate the controlled vocabulary used for the values in the <genre> element.

ACDC Usage Guidelines
ACDC takes its genre terms from the Getty's Art and Architecture Thesaurus (AAT)[1] and, to a much lesser extent, the Library of Congress Thesaurus for Graphic Materials (TGM).[2]

First consult the spreadsheet on the I:drive that contains all genre terms used in MODS records to date.[3] Values should be as specific as possible, however, if a slightly broader term has already been used it may be preferable to assign that term.

If a term is found in the AAT with a parenthetical qualifier, e.g. Charts (graphic drawings), check the TGM to see if the term appears there without a qualifier. If the definition/scope note are equivalent, use the TGM term. ACDC prefers the use of terms without qualifiers because they are less awkward and more like natural language.

New terms used can be added to the spreadsheet and should be highlighted for review.

<u>Examples</u>

Cut-paper silhouette
<mods:genre authority="tgm">Cut-paper works</mods:genre>
Clipping of a newspaper wedding announcement
<mods:genre authority="aat">Wedding announcements</mods:genre>
<mods:genre authority="tgm">Clippings</mods:genre>
Receipt for purchase of books
<mods:genre authority="aat">Receipts (financial records)</mods:genre>

[1] http://www.getty.edu/research/tools/vocabularies/aat/
[2] http://www.loc.gov/pictures/collection/tgm/
[3] <u>GenreTerms.xls</u>

Figure 5.2. Sample entry from Amherst College Library's ACDC MODS Implementation Guidelines.

to rely on the archives staff to answer questions as they arose. This became easier once it was clear that everyone in the department was very responsive to being consulted, sometimes several times a day, even when they were not directly involved in the digitization projects. For example, while the staff was working on the Hitchcock materials, questions arose related to various natural history collections at the college that evolved first into "cabinets" and eventually, in some cases, into campus museums. Staff members from the archives were able to provide history about the collections and buildings in question, saving the metadata creators from doing extensive research and enabling them to quickly determine appropriate access points.

We will continue to explore ways of addressing the disparity between the pace of digitization and metadata creation. In the short term, we continue to have both graduate student interns from the local MLIS program and a member of the Technical Services staff do the bulk of the metadata creation, but discussions are also under way regarding long-term planning for metadata support. As the workloads of staff in Technical Services continue to shift, we anticipate training more people to do metadata creation. Even without specialized knowledge related to archival description, Technical Services staff members are good candidates for training because of their familiarity with cataloging standards in general and the attention to detail required by their current work in Technical Services. An added benefit to investing time in this kind of training is that there is very little turnover with our permanent staff. Our graduate student interns may initially require less training but inevitably and fittingly will leave us to begin their professional careers.

We've also learned to seek out examples from other organizations engaged in digitizing archival collections. As we work with new types of material or formats and encounter new issues, we consult with our collaborators within the library but also look to other digital archival collections to see how similar issues have been handled. Initially, we spent a good deal of time looking at the University of Massachusetts Amherst's Credo digital collections because they include item-level descriptions of archival materials encoded in MODS,[17] and the UMass Amherst Libraries' Department of Special Collections and University Archives has made their MODS Guidelines available.[18] In addition to this general review of practices from other digital archival collections, we continue to seek out sample metadata records from other institutions when specific questions arise. For example, our Buildings and Grounds Collection contains a large number of photographs, many of which capture the same subject and some of which are nearly identical. This raised questions about the best way to create titles for similar objects and how to distinguish between them in a way that would be clear and useful for researchers. Because the standards in use give little guidance on this issue, it has been helpful to scan other digital archival collections to identify the different approaches others have taken and to try to get a sense of best practice. We are always on the lookout for additional posted application profiles and supporting documentation, which allow us to draw on the experience of those whose digital archival collections were started before ours. This has been incredibly useful, and in return we are committed to sharing our documentation as a contribution toward the development of best practices for item-level description of digitized archival materials.[19]

We feel that our least acceptable compromise thus far, given our commitment to following best practices, was the creation of metadata records for the Dickinson collection that did not include all of our required data elements. However, our hope is that in the future an opportunity will arise that will allow for enhancement of those records to meet our standards and benefit researchers. In particular, we hope to draw on the expertise of Dickinson scholars and possibly collaborate with other institutions that hold Dickinson manuscripts. Those in the archives, who have worked with Emily Dickinson scholars for years, know that ascribing dates to the materials can be contentious, and all involved agreed that awaiting the possibility of scholarly input was far preferable to the alternative of including in our metadata records dates that are widely disputed. While we feel that the importance of the Dickinson materials warrants revisiting and enhancing the metadata in the future, we recognize that the absence of a required element might not be as significant for other collections and that this kind of compromise reflects a flexibility that we think will be necessary in the future in order to move projects forward quickly and make our materials widely accessible.

We continue to refine various specific aspects of metadata creation as we gain experience. For example, because there is a lack of clarity around dates in parts of every collection we've worked on and the MODS structure is better suited to concrete dates than uncertain ones, we've decided to use a note field specifically for dates in cases where the data that appears in the <dateCreated> element needs clarification:

```
<mods:note type="date" displayLabel="Date Note">Dates provided
are based on the time period during which photo engraving was in
common use, from the late 1800s to the mid-1900s.</mods:note>
```

Although this information could be included in a general note, we think that separating it from other general note information and clearly identifying which element it refers to makes for a more easily understood display for the user. It is almost certain that additional unforeseen issues will arise as we handle new collections with new types of material, but we believe we have established a solid foundation on which to build. As we adjust and refine our procedures, we plan to keep our posted documentation current.

Although we have definitely learned that the work of item-level description of archival materials is time intensive, we are convinced of the benefit of rich metadata and plan to continue to develop tools to support efficient metadata creation so we don't have to sacrifice granularity. That said, we do weigh resources and time with the needs of our users and make decisions accordingly. The Classroom Charts are an example of a situation where, with more time and effort, we could have supplied additional or richer metadata. Instead, we concluded that the metadata we were able to provide seemed sufficient to allow good access to the materials and there wasn't a compelling reason, such as international scholarly interest in the collection, to invest the added resources. On the other hand, when discussing the Buildings and Grounds Collection with Mike, we determined that including building names as access points in our records was essential to the user. Because there are no existing authority records for these headings, we will have to invest time in establishing authorized forms of the building names. We decided it was worth the investment in time and effort not just to improve access to this collection but also because these headings will very likely be used in the future for other collections and possibly for additional projects related to the not-too-distant bicentennial of the founding of Amherst College.

The best advice we can give to others in a similar situation is this: Be genuinely open to collaboration; work closely together in the early stages to ease the transition for all involved; identify areas of expertise and interest; meet and talk early and often; and document all decisions, no matter how seemingly mundane. And consider sharing application profiles and documentation as a contribution to the community of librarians creating digital archival collections.

CONCLUSION

As our metadata program evolves, we will continue to try to balance the cost of the resources necessary to support our investment in metadata creation against the benefit that metadata will provide to our current and future users. To make well-informed choices, we will need data: statistics on the time required to create metadata records; user analytics from ACDC; and input directly from our users gathered through qualitative methods, such as usability testing. We will also review new and changing standards and guidelines as they emerge to determine how they might influence our practices. Since we began our work two years ago, DACS has undergone a full revision, DCRM(G) has been completed and approved by the Library of Congress Policy and Standards Division, and DCRM(MSS) continues to develop.

We plan to work with our Information Technology department to develop interfaces that take further advantage of our structured metadata and add the infrastructure for additional collections. ACDC already uses our granular metadata to enable the faceted browsing that allows users to refine search results, but we hope to add the ability to analyze our collections through geographical, chronological, and concept mapping interfaces. We are also working with other units in the college, such as the

Beneski Museum of Natural History, to develop metadata practices for their content and incorporate their collections into ACDC.

It can be easy to focus on all of the things we have yet to do and forget to celebrate how far we've come. Two and a half years ago there was no digitization lab, no coordinated approach to metadata for digital collections, and no written guidelines for these efforts. Our work has been a positive model of effective cross-departmental collaboration and retooling of skills, and the combination of archival knowledge and cataloging expertise has resulted in richer data for our users. Most importantly, our metadata program, along with the digitization of the materials themselves, has significantly enhanced and expanded access to important collections of unique and rare materials.

Kelcy Shepherd *is head of digital programs and* ***Kate Gerrity*** *is cataloging librarian at the Amherst College Library.*

NOTES

1. "Open Access Initiative Protocol for Metadata Harvesting," accessed August 29, 2013, www.openarchives.org/pmh/.
2. Library of Congress, "Metadata Object Description Schema Official Website," accessed August 29, 2013, www.loc.gov/standards/mods/.
3. DLF Aquifer Metadata Working Group, "Digital Library Federation/Aquifer Implementation Guidelines for Shareable MODS Records, Version 1.1," accessed August 29, 2013, https://wiki.dlib.indiana.edu/download/attachments/24288/DLFMODS_ImplementationGuidelines.pdf.
4. Society of American Archivists, *Describing Archives: A Content Standard,* viii, 209.
5. *Describing Archives: A Content Standard,* 8.
6. Rare Books and Manuscripts Section Bibliographic Standards Committee, "DCRM(MSS): Descriptive Cataloging of Rare Materials (Manuscripts)," accessed August 29, 2013, www.rbms.info/committees/bibliographic_standards/dcrm/dcrmmss/dcrmmss.html.
7. Rare Books and Manuscripts Section Bibliographic Standards Committee, "DCRM(G): Descriptive Cataloging of Rare Materials (Graphics)," accessed August 29, 2013, www.rbms.info/committees/bibliographic_standards/dcrm/dcrmg/dcrmg.html.
8. Amherst College, "Amherst College Digital Collections," accessed August 29, 2013, https://acdc.amherst.edu/.
9. Emily Dickinson, *The Poems of Emily Dickinson,* ed. Thomas H. Johnson (Cambridge, Mass.: Belknap Press of Harvard University Press, 1955).
10. "Dickinson Electronic Archives," accessed September 2, 2013, www.emilydickinson.org/.
11. "The Consecrated Eminence: A Peep into the Archives & Special Collections of Amherst College," accessed September 2, 2013, http://consecratedeminence.wordpress.com/.
12. Open Knowledge Foundation, "The Public Domain Review: Curator's Choice," accessed September 2, 2013, http://publicdomainreview.org/curators-choice/.
13. "Digital Commonwealth: Massachusetts Collections Online," accessed August 29, 2013, www.digitalcommonwealth.org/.
14. OCLC, "OAIster: Find the Pearls," accessed August 29, 2013, http://oaister.worldcat.org/.
15. "schema.org," accessed August 29, 2013, http://schema.org/.

16. Example metadata record showing required elements.
17. "credo," accessed August 29, 2013, http://credo.library.umass.edu/.
18. Special Collections and University Archives, University of Massachusetts Amherst, "Guidelines for Implementing MODS," accessed August 29, 2013, http://credo.library.umass.edu/SCUAMODSGuidelines2012.pdf.
19. Amherst College Library, "ACDC MODS Implementation Guidelines," accessed September 3, 2013, www.amherst.edu/system/files/media/ACDCMODSGuidelines.pdf.

SIX

A Long Road

Creating Policies and Procedures for Mandatory Arrangement and Description by Records Creators

Kristjana Kristinsdóttir,
National Archives of Iceland

In 1985 new legislation was passed on the National Archives of Iceland (NAIS). An innovation in the National Archives Act was the requirement that the NAIS was to supervise archiving by the state and to issue guidelines on it. This meant that for the first time the NAIS was able to make rules regarding the compilation and handling of records by state institutions. Before this, the NAIS had only been a repository for old records from state institutions. The provisions referred to here are in Article 6 of the act, which concern the deposit requirement and the obligation to comply with the NAIS's requirements on final arrangement of records. These read as follows:

> Records subject to the legal deposit requirement shall normally be made over to the National Archives not later than when they are thirty years old. . . . The directors of institutions under the legal deposit requirement are responsible for archiving within the institutions. Parties under the legal deposit requirement shall comply with the National Archives' directions on registration, sorting and final arrangement of the records.[1]

In this case study, I describe the procedures we developed for describing archives and how they evolved in the course of my work, first for a ministerial archiving committee and later as an employee of the National

Archives of Iceland. Following the passage of the National Archives Act, we faced an enormous challenge because of the huge backlog of materials held by the ministries and their affiliated institutions, a large percentage of which were overdue to be deposited in the NAIS, and all of which needed to be properly arranged and described. Processing all these records and making them ready for public access was far beyond the limited resources of the NAIS. Our response was perhaps a shocking one: The ministries and institutions belonging to them would themselves be required to take responsibility for undertaking this processing, conforming to standards and practices developed by the National Archives. Implementing this requirement was not a smooth process, but now, 20 years later, I believe we succeeded in creating a culture in which for the most part the ministries and institutions belonging to them accept their responsibilities and cooperate with us effectively.

PLANNING

It should be mentioned here that the same year that the new act was passed, the NAIS acquired new premises that made it possible to receive new record deposits. Our previous premises had long been full and no deliveries of records had been able to take place for many years. At that time, the NAIS had a staff of 12, in addition to the national archivist, and the quantity of records in its holdings ran to more than seven shelf-kilometers, covering 800 years of history.

The first step after the act was passed was the appointment of a ministerial archiving committee, that is, a committee entrusted with setting rules on archiving and introducing improved records management procedures in what were then the 13 government ministries. Nothing of this type had ever been done previously. The committee consisted of the national archivist and three representatives from the ministries, including two former permanent secretaries. The committee began work in 1987, and I was appointed its special employee. This committee operated until 1989, and in 1991 *The Handbook of Record Management for the Ministries of Iceland* was printed as a result of the committee's work.

What struck me immediately at the outset of my work with the committee was that there were no descriptive inventories of the records stored in the ministries, and the records themselves were arranged in the storage archives in a variety of ways, none of which was of an acceptable standard. No guidelines existed regarding the description and arrangement of records. As few deliveries of legal deposit material had been made to the NAIS in the past (and none in recent years), the ministries' storerooms were full and the records were in urgent need of being described, put in an accessible arrangement, and made over to the NAIS, since 90 percent of records over 30 years old are kept and are to be deposited there by law. Only a very small fraction of the ministries' older records were already in the NAIS. As Iceland's first ministries were set up in 1904, the oldest material had long since been due for delivery to the archives. Of the material that had been deposited, most was from the first half of the century, but it had been selected in a very haphazard manner.

In about 1981 a rough check was made of the quantity of material still to be deposited by the ministries and other state bodies, and it was found that there were about 5,300 shelf-kilometers of unsorted records. This figure was by no means complete, however, since many institutions—including the health, justice, and educational systems and cultural bodies—were not included in the survey. Of this figure, about 1.6 shelf-kilometers held by the ministries were already due for deposit, or about to become so.[2]

The role of the ministerial archiving committee was to make a survey of the state of affairs in the ministries' preservation of records and make proposals for improvements. It was decided to take two ministries, the Ministry of Social Affairs and the Office of the Prime Minister, and use them for an experiment. In addition to reorganizing day-to-day records management in these two organizations, one of our first tasks was to examine the ministries' storerooms and describe the material there that was due for deposit in the NAIS.

Materials stored in the Ministry of Social Affairs covered the period from 1946 to 1985. The task of cataloging was planned and carried out by me and another archivist from the National Archives, in consultation with the ministry's archivist. The records were taken to the NAIS and the actual work was done in its storerooms.

Together with work on description, we compiled guidelines on the handling and description of the ministries' records. These were the first description guidelines written in Iceland covering all aspects of archival description. They were based on the original principle of provenance rules, which started being applied in Iceland in 1905. Each archive is kept separate and its internal order is respected when it is arranged. In this way, the value of the archive as a historical source, and of its individual records, is preserved. When the guidelines were prepared, attention was also given to comparable guidelines from Denmark and Sweden. The guidelines now also draw on the International Council on Archives' (ICA) General International Standard Archival Description [ISAD(G)] and International Standard Archival Authority Record (ISARR) standards.

In addition to these written guidelines, a descriptive inventory was created using FileMaker software. First, a data entry form was set up, including the name of the ministry, the year of deposit in the NAIS, the years covered by each entry/file, the filing plan of each file (where appropriate), an ID number of the series to which the records belong, and a summary of the file contents. It was possible to make printouts by box number, contents, and classification system. At this time, the computer was a new tool in the archives, and the registration of descriptive inventories in computers was also something new.

When the Ministry of Social Affairs' archives had been described, work began on those of the Office of the Prime Minister. This was done for the most part in the office itself, and I worked at it alone. The archive consisted mainly of records from 1924, when the office was established, until 1985–1990. As with the materials from the Ministry of Social Affairs, description was completed in 1989, though an addition to the archives was described later on, in 1994. These two deposits contained some records that, being less than 30 years old, were not strictly due for deposit, and this applied to certain other deposits made by the government ministries at that time.

When description of materials from these two ministries was complete, work began in other ministries, with staff from the NAIS involved directly in description. The archive of the Ministry of Education, Culture, and Science was described by two NAIS staff, and the greater part of this work was finished in 1989. The holdings of the Ministry of Fisheries were completed in 1994. Also in 1994, the records of the Ministry of Commerce were described by an NAIS employee, the introduction to the description forming part of his history course at the University of Iceland.

The archives of the Ministry of Finance were also described by an NAIS employee. A new feature in this instance was that after the work was well underway, the ministry agreed to pay the wages of the NAIS employee; this approach had never been discussed previously. That the ministry, as the office of origin, shared the costs of the processing of the archives was something completely new, and was the first step toward involving record creators in the description of their holdings. It was not introduced without some difficulty, and part of the reason the Ministry of Finance agreed to it was that its holdings constituted the largest deposit delivered to the National Archives at the time, the materials spanning the years 1904–1985. The transfer of the materials freed a lot of storage space at the ministry and so was of great advantage to it. This sharing of costs extended only to wages, and the NAIS bore all expenses relating to boxes and working facilities.

It was obvious that having the office of origin share in the costs, whether it was a government ministry or other government body, would be critical to our ability to accept all the records due for transfer to the NAIS and also that the staff of those institutions must be brought into the processes of arrangement and description. I have already mentioned the number of shelf-kilometers of records that our survey had found were stored without proper description in the various institutions. At the most, three employees of the NAIS were involved in the work of attempting to process them prior to deposit, I and two others, and we had various other tasks in addition to description—for example, introducing/installing modern records management in the ministries and other individual institutions.

As I have stated, it was obvious that the task of arranging the materials held by the state was beyond the powers of the NAIS's employees alone. Storage at many institutions was in a critical state, all space being already full of records without a proper description, which were of value as 20th-century historical sources yet were completely inaccessible to researchers and also the staff of the institutions when they were needed for their work. Furthermore, in some cases the records were essential for establishing the rights of individuals, and by law they were entitled to have access to them. The employees of the NAIS came up with two options to offer ministries, the second one inspired by the agreement reached with the Ministry of Finance. Starting in 1991, the directors of state institutions were offered a choice: either they were to handle description themselves or they were to entrust it to the NAIS in return for a fee.

IMPLEMENTATION

In 1993–1994, when we considered asking the office of origin to shoulder the financial burden for arranging and describing their records, there was not a general recognition that the institutions themselves would have to take a share in the work. Despite this, efforts were made to have government institutions and ministries commit resources to the preparation of their materials for deposit. Fortunately, this had already started to some degree in the ministries we had already been working with, in which their archivists shared in developing descriptions. A manual on records management for institutions published in 1995 outlined two options for the heads of the government institutions:

1. The institution's own staff will see to description and arrangement, using description guidelines from the NAIS, with visits by specialists from the NAIS during the execution of the work.
2. A cost estimate will be drawn up, covering the cost of boxes and wages for a staff member. The archive will be transferred, without a proper description, to the NAIS, which will see to description in return for a fee as assessed.[3]

The cost estimates made at the outset were based on minimum costs: The working time required for each shelf-meter was kept to a minimum and attempts were made to make still further reductions rather than to make the fee reflect actual costs. In the beginning, this was done in order to encourage the institutions to take their share in the description and arrangement costs since they were not used to the idea of paying for such work. Thus, each shelf-meter was estimated as taking a maximum of 8 hours, instead of the actual 16 hours that would have to be allowed, in view of the state of the material at the time, to complete the arrangement and make a printed descriptive inventory available. Thus, in reality there was always some cost in connection with each archive received without a proper description, and this was borne by the NAIS.

In the long run, therefore, this approach (option 2) was not acceptable. Also, it frequently happened that as a result of the cost estimates it was decided to postpone the work or not to go ahead with it at all. It was considered far too expensive, running in some cases to millions of Icelandic krónur—that is, several times the monthly wage of a civil servant. Some felt no need to pay for something that could be put off, and there was no penalty for holding onto the records and not transferring them. Another problem with the option of having creators pay for the work was that often materials that had been deposited at the National Archives under these terms piled up and lay untouched for a long time, even a year or more, until work began on arranging them. No additional staff had been taken on to process the deposited material, and there were plenty of other tasks to be attended to, such as preparing guidelines on day-to-day records management in the institutions; these tasks were handled by the same employees who were responsible for the descriptive project.

It also happened that if an institution was abolished (something that was by no means uncommon around 1995), its entire record holdings were made over to the NAIS, after which an application for funding was made to the ministry responsible for it, and the ministry was then obliged to pay the cost of processing the records. In practice, this often meant that young people were engaged on a temporary basis to arrange and describe the materials, but these people lacked any experience in the field. The result was that the permanent NAIS staff sometimes had to take on the time-consuming task of training and guiding the new recruits so as to ensure that the job was done properly. Even with this training, the results were mixed, and in some cases a lot of work was needed afterward to correct mistakes, including typing errors made in entries in the computer system. All of the finishing steps connected with the processing, such as sticking labels on boxes, proofreading inventories, and so on, were another time-consuming burden on the NAIS staff that wasn't accounted for or supported by the ministry's financial contribution.

Because of all these difficulties, in 1997–1998, the rule was changed so that the only option for creating bodies, with rare exceptions, was that the work be done in the institutions before the materials were deposited. In this way it was possible to monitor procedures and make demands from a distance and also to examine the results before the deposit was made and to have things corrected where necessary. Having each institution carry out its own descriptive work could also work out better for the institutions themselves, as they would be able to spread the cost over a longer period.

Several requirements had to be met so as to make it possible for description and arrangement to be completed in the institutions before the records were deposited in the NAIS. First, approval had to be given by the director of the institution for this new expenditure, meaning that the director had to recognize the need for the work to be done. In practice, at that time directors were by no means all equally well disposed toward giving priority to a project of this type, even when the records in their storage rooms were long due for deposit (well over 30 years old). There has been a gradual change in attitudes, however, and now, more than 20 years later, it is accepted as normal practice to arrange the archives in the institutions themselves under the guidance of a member of the NAIS staff.

Another requirement is that good guidelines must be available on the arrangement and description of archives to guide the work. As has been mentioned above, the emphasis in compiling our first set of guidelines was on compliance with the principle of provenance. The guidelines have been revised as necessary since then, and we found that it was difficult to write guidelines on processing in such a way as to ensure that they would be interpreted in the same way by different people. The guidelines cover description of archives in general and therefore they deal with fairly obvious things such as placing record files in boxes and recording the box contents in the inventory. The fact is that it was possible to misunderstand the guidelines in an incredible number of ways even though the NAIS staff tried their best to make them clear. Examples of areas of misunderstanding include the need to label folders in numerical order when more than one fits into a box, labeling of boxes in numerical order within series but not within the whole collection, and confusion about the necessity of throwing away plastic sleeves, paper clips, and rubber bands that can harm the documents. To help address these issues, courses on archival requirements were also put on for persons in charge of the project in each institution, and for the staff who actually carried out the work. Many such courses were held and were well attended and are still held at present.

At first, the guidelines were sent to the institutions either by fax or in the form of computer printouts sent by post. Special guidelines were also compiled for district commissioners in whose keeping there are many records that individuals may need to access in order to assert their rights, for example, regarding property. Special guidelines were also compiled for lawyers in connection with records relating to bankruptcy estates. Besides the printed form, all these guidelines are available on the Internet, as are the ordinary ones; computer technology was adopted for this purpose at the first opportunity in the years around 1990.

In an effort to make things easier for the people in the creating agencies and to help enforce our guidelines, in 1994–1995 a standard inventory was set up in the FileMaker program (similar to the one we had developed for processing the records of the Ministry of Social Affairs) that was designed to be of use to everyone. The advantage of this program was that it was easy to learn, and it was also cheap enough to be within the institutions' budgets. Unfortunately, we did not know that at the time FileMaker was only available for Macintosh computers, so PC owners were not able to use it initially; instead, they had to use Excel or similar programs to make inventories of their archives, recording the information on each file in accordance with the NAIS's guidelines. It was not until some years later that FileMaker was available for PC computers, and so everyone was able to use the standard inventory file we had created. To begin with, each institution had to purchase the program, but it is now available in a run-time version on the NAIS's website. Thus, technological developments have been of great value in this project and influenced its progress.

There is one more thing that played a major part in achieving a positive outcome: one-to-one guidance provided by staff of the NAIS on the arrangement and description of individual archives. Before NAIS staff visit the institutions, guidelines are sent out and the institutions' workers are expected to acquaint themselves with them as well as they can. Then when someone from the NAIS visits the institution, he or she goes over the guidelines point by point and the worker is able to ask in detail about anything that is unclear. Directions are given on grouping records according to series, and suggestions are given as to which series would be best to start on when making the inventory. Methods of description and boxing records are demonstrated, and a start is made on entering data into the program. After this, the institution's worker is welcome to contact the NAIS whenever necessary if problems arise. When the institutions are located in Reykjavík, where the NAIS is based, we arrange a visit to provide instruction. This is normally done by phone when institutions are far outside the metropolitan area. Attempts were made to have regional archives provide guidance, but this was abandoned and it has generally proved better to send someone from the NAIS to the places in question if more help is needed or to complete final processing when the records are sent to Reykjavík. This kind of long-distance assistance applies almost exclusively to district commissioners' archives. The district commissioners' offices are spread throughout the country but are obliged by law to deposit their archive materials in the NAIS and not in the regional archives.

To be able to launch this project and set the procedures in place, it was necessary that the staff of the NAIS should have knowledge of modern records management and archival arrangement, since we were responsible for the success of the project. And as I have already mentioned, the legislative changes resulted in many other new tasks to be dealt with too, so while the staff were happy to have their mandate expanded and supported, it placed a considerable burden on them. Another challenge of this new approach was that many of those who were engaged by the ministries and institutions for the descriptive work were students during their summer vacations or else older permanently employed people who wanted to reduce their working hours. As discussed above, all training and guidance was provided by staff of the NAIS, who also needed to devote part of their time to reviewing work products and finalizing the processing after deposit.

In the new operations model, NAIS was responsible for putting forward draft estimates of the overall costs for arranging and describing the material. Cost estimates were based on the projected costs of both wages for staff and boxes for the volume of materials to be addressed. Frequently, these wage cost estimates were calculated based on the wages of a newly qualified student and the number of hours needed to cover each shelf-meter (generally taken as six to eight hours); it was assumed that each meter would require 12 boxes, this being based on a particular type of box that the institutions were recommended to buy and that in fact was the only type available in Iceland. Attempts were made to make realistic estimates—that is, not according to the highest possible standards yet also ensuring that at least minimum standards would be observed at all times. The highest possible standards would involve the compilation of a detailed introduction covering the history of the institution and descriptions of individual series and of the individual records and the archive as a whole. The minimum requirement was that the records be arranged in boxes, these being ordered according to the series and cataloged in the NAIS's catalog format. To begin with, it was not envisaged that boxes and file jackets be replaced or that records be placed inside acid-free folders. This was not required until later, in approximately 1998–1999, since there were no acid-free boxes or folders available until then in Iceland.

Currently, before deposit, random samples are taken from the processed material and checked to ensure that everything has been done properly and that the contents of boxes correspond to the entries in the inventory. After deposit has taken place, the inventory is checked thoroughly against the deposited material in the NAIS and, following correction where necessary, the inventory is put on the Internet for public access. However, despite our best efforts to provide guidelines and training, often the archival descriptions are not all done satisfactorily, and the policy is for the NAIS not to accept archives unless minimum standards are met. If standards are not met, the records are not accepted until they comply with the minimum standards. In some cases, description of the materials is amended at the NAIS and the record-creating body is then billed accordingly.

Since we began implementing this approach starting in 1991 and then with modifications in 1993–1994, at the most, only two or three NAIS staff members were involved in developing the guidelines and the FileMaker inventory, training staff and student workers, providing additional assistance and guidance, and inspecting deposits to ensure they met the minimum standards. Although the policy is that all work must be done by the record-creating office, occasionally the NAIS does receive individual deposits for description in the NAIS, the work being paid for by the institution. No exemptions are now made from the requirements for physical processing; for example, all files must be submitted in acid-free folders and boxes. Information is also required on the institution submitting the materials—when it was founded, its directors, responsibilities, and so forth—to assist us in creating the description. Information is also submitted on each series, contents of the records, and their years of origin. All this is in accordance with the ICA's standards.

RESULTS

After our initial troubles in making heads of institutions accept their responsibilities and in training their staff to meet our standards, the whole exercise has now met with approval all round. For archivists at the NAIS, the visible result is that archive materials all over the country are being put in order and so made available for use. We are the ones who are responsible for ensuring that things are done properly and in accordance with the rules set by the NAIS. We do not have to do every single part of the work ourselves, yet the records come in properly arranged and described and therefore more accessible. It has become less and less common now to come across whole storerooms full of records going back 30–100 years. For directors of institutions, it is important to know that they are in compliance with the law on archives. Each one of them is individually responsible for the records in their institutions; recognition of this responsibility and what is involved has been growing, though there is still a long way to go. For users, the results of the project are that archives are now being properly described and made accessible for research far more quickly than used to be the case, in addition to which this accessibility is important for the general public in connection with people's right to information.

One result that can be assessed is that it is now recognized that the NAIS's rules and guidelines on archival description and arrangement must be followed, and its procedures are generally accepted by those state institutions that are required to deposit their archive materials. They must all describe their archives in accordance with the NAIS's rules, which are displayed on its home page and accessible to everyone, in addition to which these rules have been published in the *Government*

Gazette. It is now the exception that records without any proper description are driven to the NAIS without any previous agreement having been made. Perhaps the most tangible result is that during the past 20 years the NAIS has accepted 1,090 accessions from government institutions amounting to a total of 14 shelf-kilometers. More than 64 percent of that, or 9 shelf-kilometers, had been described by the institutions before the accession took place.

LESSONS LEARNED

As is clear from the lengthy history in this narrative, it took many years to explore different models and policies for efficiently arranging and describing these government records, as well as to establish a culture in which our requirements were commonly accepted. It was interesting and challenging, as it had no precedent, and after some teething troubles it now runs smoothly on the whole and is fully accepted today. Not everything went without a hitch, however; many heads of institutions were appalled at the costs they were required to pay to have "dusty" records, which they regarded as irrelevant and forgotten, taken out of their storerooms and subjected to archival description and arrangement. They felt it was demeaning to have to submit to the rules set by the NAIS staff, and thought they were being unreasonable and officious; they saw it as of no concern to anyone but themselves how these records were kept.

It sometimes happened that the NAIS found a delivery van on its car park, piled high with unsorted records that had simply been piled into the van in no order. The NAIS had not been contacted or warned in advance of the delivery. This often called for sensitive negotiations with the van driver to get him to drive his cargo back to where it had come from, and then a heated discussion with the head of the institution to make him or her understand that this was not the way records were to be delivered to the National Archives. They had to take the materials back in the same condition as they had sent them. It could take a long time to sort such misunderstandings out, but in the end agreement was reached and the records were properly processed. Other heads of institutions were more amenable and were only too glad to have their archives accessible and in good order. They also realized the advantage in being able to know whether it was possible to get rid of some of the material in their storerooms and so gain more space. However, it took at least 10 years before the good sense of our requirements were widely acknowledged and most ministers understood that a good description of archives was an inherent part of a proper management of an institution.

For the success of this project, legal support was important. The National Archives Act of 1985 states that ministries and institutions belonging to them shall comply with NAIS's rules on describing and arranging archives. This clause has proved to be extremely important in implementing this method and also in achieving recognition of the importance of the project on the part of the directors of institutions and other authorities. It should also be mentioned here that having the institutions describe and arrange their archives, with aid and guidance provided by the NAIS, has proved to be a better option than having them pay for that work done by the NAIS. It gives the institutions the flexibility of distributing the inherent cost and scheduling the work as they see fit. When unprepared archives were delivered to the NAIS with an agreement of the institution paying the cost, the archives tended to pile up since there was no staff to do the description work. That approach has therefore been dropped (except in very rare cases) and the NAIS has now a special staff member to deal with those cases. For archives wanting to explore establishing similar policies, we think it is critical to prepare the best possible guidelines on arrangement and description that you can but also be prepared to follow up with one-on-one training. Time must be allotted for staff to be able to give guidance to the institutions and make sure that the work goes ahead. You should also look into all aspects of the materials and facilities necessary, such as boxes and other supplies, to make sure they meet the requirements. These steps will ensure that the outcome will be properly ordered archives with inventories that open up access to scholars and others.

CONCLUSION

The National Archives Act of 1985 formed the legal framework necessary for implementing the policy of requiring ministries and institutions to conduct arrangement and description of their own records. However, the 1991 decision of the Ministry of Finance to pay for the description and arrangement of its archives was also important because it paved the way for other ministries to do the same. It showed recognition of the responsibility of a record-creating body by having their staff take an active part in the description work and by contributing to the work done by NAIS. This demonstrated commitment was part of the evolution of our policies that led us to have the ability to require that government institutions do the description work themselves.

Guides on archival description and arrangement have been issued, and the method that proved successful was included in *Records Management for Institutions: A Manual* (1995). Since then it has been the standard practice that description and arrangement has been completed when archives are delivered to the NAIS. This was not easy to begin with since the directors of government institutions were reluctant, but now this practice is taken for granted. Looking back over more than 20 years, I can honestly say that the result of our efforts has been remarkable. Now, government institutions fully grasp the benefits of describing their archives without delay. This practice strengthens daily handlings of documents as well as later disposition. Archives without a proper description do not pile up any more. Instead, delivered materials are immediately accessible for research. Working procedures are, of course, capable of constant improvement. But we have made great progress, and the rules and guidelines are now available on the NAIS's website. Courses are held regularly, demonstrating and examining the procedures. We plan to produce a short video of certain parts of the procedure and to make it available on the NAIS's website. This would relieve the NAIS staff of some of the burden of answering repetitive questions. More varieties of acid-free boxes are now available to choose from, and constant work is being done on improving the range. Altogether, the project has been successful and is working very efficiently.

Kristjana Kristinsdóttir *is archivist at the National Archives of Iceland and Lector in Archival Studies at the University of Iceland.*

NOTES

1. Alþingi. Lög um Þjóðskjalasafn Íslands nr. 66/1985 (National Archives Act, No. 66/1985), trans. Jessfrey Cosser and Benedikt Jónsso.
2. ÞÍ. Skjalasafn menntamálaráðuneytis 1999-78-B-B/370-1, Álit skjalavörslunefndar, September 1981, s. 34–35. (The Archives of the Ministry of Education, Culture and Science. Opinion of the Archiving Committee.)
3. Kristjana Kristinsdóttir, *Skjalavarsla stofnana, Handbók* (Records Management for Institutions: A Manual) (Reykjavík: Þjóðskjalasafn Íslands, 1995), 32.

SEVEN

Collaboration in Cataloging

Sourcing Knowledge from Near and Far for a Challenging Collection

Evyn Kropf, University of Michigan

Every repository has collections that present descriptive challenges, particularly for detailed, item-level description. When the linguistic, subject, and methodological expertise required for examining and characterizing the contents and physical features of the items is lacking among the staff of the repository, it is only natural to seek that expertise elsewhere. Depending on the complexity of the materials, sometimes the full complement of needed expertise can be found in a single scholar, who can be called upon to contribute to cataloging. All too often, though, no such appropriately skilled scholar can be found (or afforded), and other options must be investigated. Additionally, the repository might want to explore channels for broader scholarly engagement with the materials, beyond a single established expert.

In such a situation, the repository has a number of options. It could hire one emerging scholar with only a measure of the requisite expertise who could then develop his or her skills to the full complement (and beyond) in the course of the descriptive project. Or it might attempt to tap wider collective expertise—perhaps by crowdsourcing elements of the description among a "crowd" of distributed scholars (potentially capable of contributing but not necessarily motivated to do so) or by hiring a whole cohort of emerging scholars (i.e., students), highly motivated and again capable of enhancing their skills (and thereby contribution potential) in the course of the project. Such collaborative approaches would have the advantage of also facilitating wider engagement with the collection while the item descriptions are still being assembled.

At the University of Michigan Library, we've had the chance to try all of the above, both deliberately and serendipitously. In 2009, we embarked on a four-year, grant-funded project to complete the cataloging of our Islamic Manuscript Collection. Building on the momentum of the crowdsourcing wave, only just beginning to sweep the cultural heritage community at the time of our grant proposal in 2008,[1] our Collaboration in Cataloging: Islamic Manuscripts at Michigan project initially attempted to "crowdsource the cataloging" by soliciting descriptive content from scholars around the world.

A small cohort of emerging scholars at the University of Michigan, freshly trained in the fundamentals of Islamicate manuscript studies and led by myself as project cataloger, was hired to handle the task of creating bibliographic records and enhancing them with the descriptive content (revised as necessary) received via crowdsourcing.

To our surprise, it was by sourcing this newly minted "local crowd" that we were able to achieve the most in terms of scholarly engagement and manuscripts cataloged (in both quality and quantity). Our attempts at harnessing the expertise of the wider remote crowd weren't wholly unsuccessful, but we found that there was still much to learn about how to apply the crowdsourcing approach to meet our descriptive goals. Although our experience creating descriptions for Islamic manuscripts called upon a very specialized skill set, I think the lessons—both positive and negative—can be applied to working with any collection for which a repository needs to harness outside expertise.

PLANNING

At the University of Michigan Library, we are fortunate to hold a sizable collection of Islamic manuscripts, chiefly in codex format and carrying texts largely in Arabic, Persian, and Ottoman Turkish. From a single copy of the Qur'an donated in 1914, our collection has grown to 1,091 volumes, 4 rolls, and 3 single leaves, placing it among the largest such collections in North America.[2]

Basic inventory cataloging for the manuscripts was carried out in varying levels of detail between 1925 and 1993. Even in 2008 the composition of the collection remained little known, with a card-format handlist—carrying limited inventory data and arranged by subcollection, language, and subject—providing the only intellectual access to most of the manuscripts. Expertise relevant to the full range of languages and subjects, not to mention the palaeographic and codicological features of the manuscripts, was lacking in the library, and resources to assemble the necessary expertise for the time required were extremely limited.

Over the years, when students with the appropriate linguistic skills had appeared at the university, the library was able to hire them and raise the level of description for some portion of the collection. In fact, by 1993, around 20 percent of the volumes were described well enough to be considered "fully cataloged" with bibliographic records in the library's online catalog and OCLC WorldCat. We had also relied on the occasional contributions of established scholars—University of Michigan faculty with appointments in the Near Eastern Studies or Art History departments and visiting scholars who had managed to hear of the collection and visit the library—to enhance the inventory descriptions for certain manuscripts with annotations on the catalog cards. In these cases, manuscripts pertaining to the special research interests of the scholars at hand were privileged for descriptive enhancement; others remained neglected. In either case, those manuscripts that did not have entries in the online catalog were largely invisible to scholars, and most inventory and descriptive information was trapped in one physical source. Clearly this was not a tenable solution for intellectual or physical control, not to speak of public access.

As we were grappling with how to address this problem, in 2008 the Council on Library and Information Resources (CLIR) announced a new grant program, generously funded by the Andrew W. Mellon Foundation, designed to address descriptive challenges such as ours. The program, Cataloging Hidden Special Collections and Archives, would offer funding to projects that exhibited potential for national impact on scholarship and teaching, proposed innovative or highly efficient approaches to description, applied standards that would ensure interoperability and long-term sustainability of data, and adopted workflow and outreach practices that maximized connections to user communities.[3]

We were inspired by our experience with digitization and sourcing descriptive contributions from scholars engaged with the Islamic Manuscripts Collection to propose our Collaboration in Cataloging project for the grant program. In keeping with the approach taken for other codex manuscripts in our Special Collections, we wished to create bibliographic records for each item that would reside in the online library catalog and be distributed more broadly via WorldCat, and chose the descriptive cataloging of Ancient, Medieval, Renaissance, and Early Modern Manuscripts (AMREMM) standard[4] as the basis for our descriptive schema.[5] Crowdsourcing—facilitated by digitization and supervised by a project cataloger—was envisioned as a means of overcoming the limitations in our local expertise. We hoped it would help us complete the cataloging more quickly, efficiently, and cost effectively while engaging scholars with the collection even before it received adequate item-level description.

In our projected workflow, preliminary bibliographic records—populated with the inventory descriptions from the catalog cards—would be created by the project cataloger and posted, along with links to digital surrogates of the manuscripts, to a project website. Next, remote crowd-sourced contributors would examine the digital surrogates, correct the existing inventory data, and supply additional descriptive details, which the project cataloger would then review, edit, and add as enhancements to the bibliographic records. The project proposal included funding for a cadre of graduate students to assist the project cataloger with bibliographic record creation and enhancement.[6]

IMPLEMENTATION

Our proposal for this iterative and dynamic descriptive collaboration was accepted by CLIR, and we began work in January 2009. The project was implemented in three phases of varying length over the course of four years. (Our initial timeline was three years, as covered by the grant award, but we were able to obtain a no-cost extension of one year in order to more fully realize project goals.)

Phase 1: Training, Record Creation, Digitization, and Website Development

The first months of the project were dedicated to hiring staff and launching the digitization effort. I came on board as project cataloger at the beginning of March 2009. At that time, I was a graduate student within a few months of completing my degree from the University of Michigan's School of Information, as well as an Arabist who had completed advanced coursework in the Near Eastern Studies department. My first task was to begin designing the workflows for bibliographic record creation and enhancement. Three cataloging assistants—all graduate students in the Department of Near Eastern Studies at the University of Michigan—joined me in May.

Also in May, the cataloging assistants and I attended a weeklong workshop conducted by Adam Gacek, a world-renowned expert in Arabic manuscript studies. Organized by one of the cataloging assistants with support from several departments and institutes on campus, the workshop was held at the university with a final hands-on session conducted with manuscripts from the collection in the university library. This workshop represented a rare and incredibly valuable opportunity to gain fundamental training in the principles of examining and describing Islamic manuscripts. Apart from a few exceptional university courses and institutes, mainly in Europe, Egypt, and Iran, such opportunities have been largely lacking from most Middle Eastern scholars' academic training.

Following the workshop and inspired by the approach of Gacek and other scholars,[7] I further elaborated our AMREMM-based descriptive schema with modifications to suit the linguistic and codicological features of the manuscripts, and defined a suite of descriptive elements that we would gather in the course of the project to achieve "full" codicological description for each manuscript.[8] I also created corresponding bibliographic record templates and workforms in digital format.

That summer, the students and I began to create the preliminary bibliographic records in MARC21 format, working from the data in the catalog cards but not examining the manuscripts themselves. I assigned catalog cards to the students and myself, dividing them up according to working pace and language ability. Into the blank workforms we transcribed the existing inventory data from the cards, supplied the corresponding vernacular in Arabic or modified Arabic script, and added notes and access points in authorized form taken from the Library of Congress authority files. The assistants were able to fill their workforms using a text editor (NotePad Pro) and to work from a digitized photocopy of the cards. They could thus work away from the library at their leisure, returning their completed workforms to me over email.

I next used the library's integrated library system (ILS) (ALEPH) cataloging module to edit and slightly enhance the completed workforms with subject analysis and to upload them to the library catalog as new bibliographic records. I also created holding records and item records in the library catalog, assigned a barcode to each manuscript, and prepared a marker carrying the shelfmark (call number) and barcode for each manuscript volume. As we completed work for every 50 or so manuscripts, I passed along a batch of barcode tags and a spreadsheet to my colleague in Special Collections, who then placed the tags in the volumes. This was to ensure that digitization for the previously uncataloged manuscripts could proceed efficiently and without delay, since barcodes were essential to that workflow. Working this way, the assistants and I were able to create records for all 871 volumes of uncataloged manuscripts in less than four months, well ahead of project schedule.

Also during that summer, the project web developer advanced her work on the project website, where (via conversion to MARCXML) the data from the newly created records would eventually be posted for correction and enhancement by the wider scholarly community in the true crowdsourcing phase of the project.[9] She and I collaborated to develop several templates of descriptive elements that would be used to display the data as an evolving description and to invite commentary on them.

Despite this progress, we learned during that same summer that, although digitization was proceeding swimmingly, technical issues were preventing the ingestion of the digitized manuscripts for deployment in the HathiTrust Digital Library. This would delay our deployment of the project website—and thus wider solicitations of contributions—for several months.

To maintain productivity and get under way with record enhancement despite the delay with digital surrogates and hence website deployment, I developed a collaborative workflow drawing on the contributions of the student assistants already committed to the project. Given that a significant number of the uncataloged manuscripts would not be digitized because of condition issues and it would thus be impossible to crowdsource descriptive enhancements for them via the project website, I decided to focus the productivity of our local crowd on them. I created a form in Google Docs that both guided the manuscript examination and description and provided a means of recording and sharing the descriptive data for consultation, feedback, editing, and eventual entry to the online catalog. I also created a database for seal impressions and other inscriptions from the manuscripts in the form of a Picassa web album, which eased transcription through visual comparison and again supported feedback on questions.

When the students returned to work in September, joined by a fourth student who had also attended the May manuscript studies workshop, I again assigned manuscripts and distributed workforms across the students and myself according to descriptive and language abilities. That fall and the following winter we made excellent progress, particularly with the Arabic manuscripts, with 81 manuscripts (25 of which the assistants had worked on) fully cataloged by the end of March 2010 when the project site was finally launched.

Training also continued. Given our focus on physical examination, in February 2010, I coordinated with the library's conservation department to arrange a multisession workshop with an external expert. Book conservator and historical bindings expert Julia Miller taught both our project cataloging staff and library conservation staff about Islamic bindings, book structures, materials, and condition.

Phase 2: Website Deployment, Record Enhancement, and Continued Digitization

Thanks to our project manager and our liaison to the Library's Digital Library Production Service, the ingest issues were finally resolved and in March 2010 we were able to formally launch the project website and thus properly enter the second and longest phase of the project, which was focused on completing digitization and ingest, and enriching the bibliographic records with descriptive contributions from the wider scholarly community via the project website. With the launch of the site in March, we issued a broad call for contributions that the principal investigator and I distributed over the major listservs used by scholars in the various fields of Middle Eastern studies.

As digitized manuscripts appeared in the HathiTrust Digital Library, I used the project website admin interface to post a description populated with the data we had entered during record creation, two representative images, and links to the full digital surrogate. I assigned categories for languages and tags for subjects to each manuscript post to facilitate finding via the public interface. Contributors could then locate manuscript descriptions of interest, follow the links to the digitized manuscripts, examine them, and offer enhancements or corrections to the existing descriptive information in the form of comments (see figure 7.1). Initially, in order to make contributing as simple as possible, contributors were required to enter only their name and email with their comment; however, by the final year of the project, I decided to require registration due to the vast amount of spam comments we had been receiving.

When contributors submitted comments, I received an email notification with the text of their comment and the name and email address they submitted along with it. In order to vet and keep track of their contributions, I would first search online to determine their institution or organization (if affiliated at all) and title, and then assign them a "role" — student, faculty, librarian, manuscript cataloger/specialist, calligrapher, etc. I recorded these details along with date and number of first comments, and date and number of subsequent comments in a spreadsheet. I would then review their comment, determine if it could be suitably incorporated into the evolving description for that manuscript, and send them an email of acknowledgment, thanking them for their contribution and inviting further contributions as well as responding to any queries. If necessary, I would gently offer them feedback in the form of correction and even instruction related to manuscript description. If the comment was acceptable, I would make a note of it in my workflow spreadsheets so that I could eventually revise it and add it to the catalog record for the manuscript along with a statement acknowledging the contributor.

In the course of the year following our website launch, we received only 36 comments from 13 contributors. The majority of these followed immediately after the call for contributions was issued. While this slim volume of responses from outside scholars was disappointing, we continued drawing from the contributions of our known local crowd in order to maintain progress with realizing full cataloging for the manuscripts. Two assistants departed the project at the end of that summer and a new assistant came on board. I continued to direct their efforts according to descriptive skill and language expertise. Thus, when full cataloging for the undigitized Arabic manuscripts was virtually complete, I began assigning them digitized manuscripts. Together the assistants had contributed to the full cataloging of 45 additional manuscripts by the end of 2010. That summer I focused my own descriptive work on digitized manuscripts and by December 2010 approximately 279 (i.e., about a third) of the previously uncataloged volumes were fully cataloged.

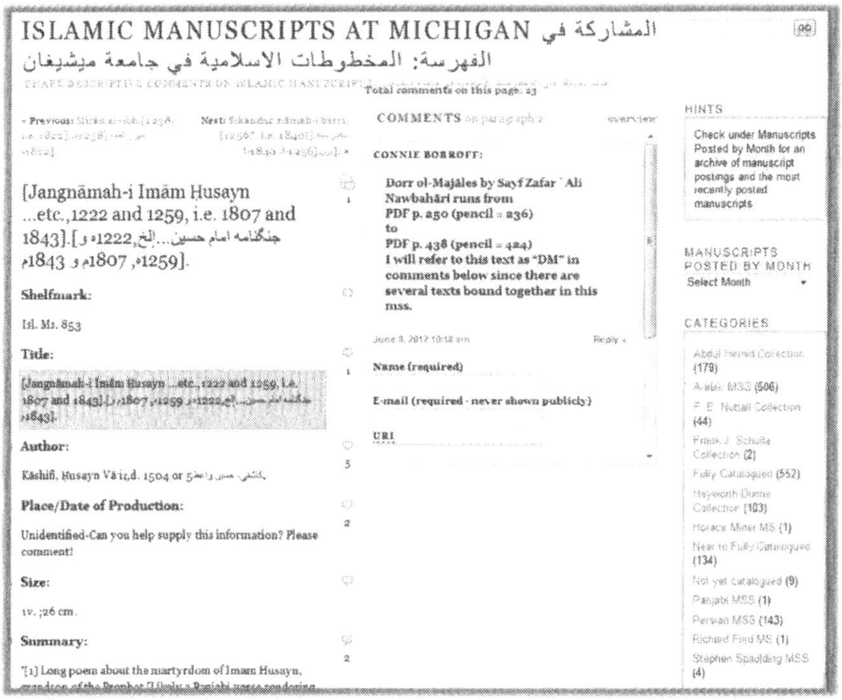

Figure 7.1. Comment submitted on a descriptive element (here the chief title) to supply information otherwise lacking.

Phase 3: A New Approach to Record Enhancement

The intended focus of the third phase had been completing the cataloging effort, broadening outreach activities, and assessing project impact and future directions. However, collaborative cataloging with outside scholars simply wasn't happening. So, in response to the limited number of remote contributions we were receiving and in the interest of seeing the greatest number of manuscripts possible cataloged by project's end, I proposed refinements to the cataloging approach that would maximize my contributions and those of my assistants while allowing us to explore a more effective means of soliciting contributions from colleagues beyond the library and the university.

In this refined approach, I was the chief source of descriptive enhancement. My work was devoted to achieving what I termed "near to full" cataloging for as many of the digitized manuscripts as possible. This involved putting off the time-consuming physical examination and producing a description of each manuscript based on what I could ascertain by examining the digital surrogate. All the while, we continued inviting descriptive contributions for the manuscripts via the project site.

I continued to utilize the skills of our cataloging assistants—two of whom had been on the project from the start, one whom I had trained the previous year, and a new Turkish specialist who, after training, was able to join me in working on the Ottoman manuscripts. Each student completed virtually full cataloging for the manuscripts assigned to him or her, with emphasis on the physical examination and manuscripts not slated for digitization.

Though accomplishing "near to full" cataloging for the collection in this way met many project goals, it did not achieve the goal of "full" cataloging that the manuscripts so richly deserved. We therefore requested and received from CLIR a no-cost extension to the project of an additional year in order to complete full cataloging for the remaining manuscripts: 539 (just over 60 percent) for which "near to full" cataloging had been achieved and 60 not yet cataloged (from those not slated for digitization).

In the course of the year, 22 colleagues made descriptive contributions via the project website, 19 who had not yet commented and 3 from among the 13 who had contributed the previous year. Their contributions were made in roughly 66 comment submissions of varying quality and richness, weighted (for long, data-rich comments) to total over 100 descriptive contributions.

This increase in volume of responses was likely a result of a deliberate effort on my part to increase project awareness in our target communities. In addition to the natural effect of more people learning about the project over time, in this year I made more frequent and more strategic calls for participation. I prepared English and Arabic versions of a project announcement and invitation for contributions, which circulated in the July 2011 issue of the journal *Chroniques du manuscrit au Yémen*. The principal investigator and I also issued another call for contributions—more targeted to specific descriptive needs this time—over the major Middle Eastern studies listservs as well as the email list of the Comparative Oriental Manuscript Studies (COMSt) research initiative.

Phase 4: Physical Examination and Description

In the final phase, made possible when CLIR approved our request for an extension, my work consisted mainly of physical examination to complete the cataloging of those manuscripts that had been "near to fully" cataloged in the previous year or had been deselected from the digitization workflow.

I continued to engage two cataloging assistants, with one virtually completing full cataloging for manuscripts assigned to him and the other (who joined the project in the fall) addressing only elements of the physical description (such as collation, pagination, dimensions, etc.). Another former assistant returned during the summer months to continue training with me on codicological description. Manuscripts not slated for digitization remained a priority for their workflow, since only through physical examination could these manuscripts be cataloged to any level.

I also found myself negotiating a happy surge in remote contributions via the project website that accompanied word of the project finally circulating among Iranian manuscript specialist colleagues. How they got word of the project is still unclear, but their enthusiastic support was most welcome.

To our immense satisfaction, this final phase concluded successfully with full cataloging completed for all of the manuscripts. I even found time to address recently acquired manuscripts, to supply enhancements to the descriptions prepared for previously "cataloged" manuscripts necessitated by researcher or class interest, and to polish and finalize all of the catalog records created and enhanced in the course of the project for export to OCLC's World Cat.

RESULTS

Our primary goal when applying for the CLIR grant had been to fully catalog and describe the manuscript collection, and in so doing encourage scholarly engagement and raise the profile of the collection. While our secondary goal of soliciting contributions from scholars around the world was less successful, we felt we had met or exceeded our primary goals.

The entire collection is now fully cataloged with richly detailed, searchable descriptions for each manuscript appearing in the online library catalog, Mirlyn. A total of 883 new catalog records were created in the course of the project, representing 1,447 titles in 877 volumes, 2 rolls, and 3 single leaves. Another 21 existing manuscript descriptions were significantly enhanced. Descriptions for the 912 digitized manuscripts appear in the HathiTrust Digital Library catalog. Descriptions for the digitized manuscripts also appear on the project website where they are exposed to search engines such as Google and thus even more accessible to researchers.

The scholarly community on campus was engaged with the project from the beginning, and because of the kinds of students the University of Michigan attracts, we were able to assemble our "local crowd" exclusively by hiring graduate students who were already on site. We hired Near Eastern Studies graduate students—four Arabists and one Persianist, as well as a couple of graduate students from the School of Information with backgrounds in Turkish and Arabic studies and strong interest in manuscript collections and processing to serve as cataloging assistants. We were able to motivate their involvement (and my own) by paying a modest amount (written into the grant) and offering an incredibly valuable educational experience for developing skills in palaeography, codicology, and manuscript description, which would have been very difficult to obtain otherwise given the current state of the education in the field.

Sourcing this local crowd for descriptive contributions and collaborative cataloging was wildly successful. Offering an emerging scholar like me the chance to develop my own existing knowledge and skills—in Islamicate history, Arabic, Persian, and Ottoman palaeography and codicological description in particular—while exercising highly proficient bibliographic, complex cataloging, and Arabic language skills—proved extremely productive. Supervising and reviewing the work of the cataloging assistants was key to this, though it did not necessarily enhance efficiency, and their contributions were incredibly valuable. Because they were on site and could therefore receive ongoing training and physically examine the manuscripts, I could rely on them to supply virtually complete descriptions and to share the time-consuming work of physical description. Their linguistic skills were also a good complement to my own, particularly early on as I was still developing my Persian palaeography.

We had less success with collaborative cataloging via the project site, and so, contrary to the expectations of the original grant, we could not rely on those contributions to generate virtually complete descriptions. In fact, for only 8 of the 696 digitized manuscripts posted did we receive contributions sufficient to compile from them a nearly complete description in the online catalog. Still, we received a couple of contributions that made a significant impact. Specifically, for a manuscript carrying Punjabi texts (which was outside the expertise of anyone on the team), remote scholars were able to assist with the identification. In the end, we received over 284 descriptive contributions from 34 scholars in Belgium, Egypt, France, Germany, Iran, Israel, Lebanon, Russia, Turkey, the United Kingdom, and the United States via our project site with the vast majority of the quality contributions being provided by two or three individuals.[10] While we were disappointed that we didn't receive more contributions from outside scholars, we considered receipt of any contributions via the project site a success, given that it represented engagement of scholars with the collection.

On campus, the project has yielded a significant increase in interest and enhanced engagement with the collection beyond the descriptive work, with many professors and instructors arranging for their classes to visit the library to view manuscripts in the course of the project. I conducted these sessions in addition to my cataloging duties. We have also seen a high volume of requests for manuscripts in the reading room.

Beyond campus, the collection of manuscripts digitized for the project (which also have their descriptive information linked to the images), "Islamic Manuscripts (Michigan)," has consistently been among the most popular HathiTrust collections, before and after the high-volume project work in Phase 3.[11] A somewhat random sampling of 25 percent of the digitized manuscripts saw a total of almost 47,000 page views between January 1, 2012, and August 8, 2013, with the most views for this selection of manuscripts coming from users in Turkey, Azerbaijan, Albania, Iraq, Hungary, Kuwait, Israel, India, Pennsylvania, Liberia, Iran, and New York.

LESSONS LEARNED

Our primary lesson was clearly that "crowdsourcing the cataloging" (in the sense of trying to source complete descriptions) or "collaborative cataloging" with remote contributors via the project site was simply not effective. Contributors tended to not cover the full range of descriptive elements but instead focused on bibliographic details pertaining to textual contents (such as title, author, subject matter, citations to relevant studies and catalogs, incipit, explicit), usually only providing a single title, citation, or transcription of incipit and explicit. Features such as decoration, layout, writing surface, and binding were almost completely neglected, although those features were included in the images provided. Contributors also tended not to address more than a few manuscripts. Less than 40 percent of contributors addressed more than one manuscript and less than 9 percent addressed more than three.

From the perspective of sourcing particular descriptive elements (not necessarily complete descriptions), even this limited response on the part of contributors could have been productive had their numbers been greater and had we been able to anticipate their preference and strategically focus our staff efforts to be complementary early on. As it turns out, our appeal did not even reach our most eager and prolific contributors, the Iranian manuscript specialists, until the final year of the project, by which time most of the descriptions were nearly complete. Their contributions were therefore only supplementary in nature, consisting mainly of variant forms of names and titles, citations to catalogs, and corrections for typos.

Were we to attempt this again, we would definitely approach things differently. Rather than trying to source a wide range of descriptive elements for a large number of manuscripts, it might be better either to limit to a small number of manuscripts beyond the expertise of local staff (if quality is desired) or to limit to a small number of descriptive elements for a larger number of manuscripts (if quantity is desired) and to tailor webforms and postings accordingly.

This would make the descriptive tasks more palatable for the contributors and the tasks of review, response, revision, and data entry more manageable for skilled staff. In reality, this crowdsourcing approach actually generates more work for staff rather than less, and if staff are sufficiently skilled, they might be able to complete the work more efficiently (and cost effectively) themselves—as we did. The appeal of crowdsourcing in these cases is scholarly engagement with the collection being described and potentially sourcing descriptive elements that staff would have found difficult or even impossible to supply unaided.

For sourcing description of specialized material such as this, the "unknown crowd" of "well-informed enthusiasts"[12] will often be very small and may be widely distributed geographically and linguistically.[13] Soliciting contributions early and often via a distributed model that leverages connections with partners in other institutions, organizations, and communities of expertise (or training) would therefore likely result in greater response than what we received in our project. These partners could help disseminate the appeal, tailoring it to language, subject expertise, specific needs and tasks, and so forth. Simply relying on academic listservs (specialized though they may be) will likely not be adequate, as some niche communities will have their own separate online forums and publications. Knowledge of scholarly networks and online channels for promotion is essential. Offering incentives beyond acknowledgment in the descriptions and advancement of a contributor's own research projects could also generate more response.

Our experience shows that while crowdsourcing information from an unknown remote crowd might not be effective for collaborative complex cataloging, developing and using a known, local crowd of subject matter specialists often will be. This may not be the most efficient approach, considering the time investment required for training, editing, and such tasks, not to mention that in some cases skilled staff might be able to perform the work more quickly. But it is absolutely invaluable for building the expertise of a group of future scholars, often in both their area of study and in work with archival or library materials. It also enhances scholarly engagement with a yet-to-be properly described (and hence otherwise relatively inaccessible) collection. This was certainly the case for our project. One of our cataloging assistants, Noah Gardiner, was able to develop in the course of his cataloging assignments his palaeographical skills and knowledge of transmission notices as evidence for scholarly networks, knowledge that has been invaluable for him in his dissertation research.

In an arrangement like ours, which utilizes students or other subject matter experts, maintaining flexibility with an iterative approach will help maximize staff contributions while contributors' skills are developing. This iterative approach can also help in making your descriptions available for crowdsourced additions, allowing for data and item discovery while the descriptions are still evolving. With all this iteration and distribution of work taking place, leveraging collaborative software—open source where possible—can help facilitate workflows with minimal investment.

For our complex descriptive tasks, sourcing via a known, local crowd better suited our time limitations, need for physical access in some cases, and goals for scholarly engagement. However, with other types of materials and descriptive methodologies, perhaps materials that have a broader pool of possible experts, the remote crowdsourcing approach might serve just as effectively, if not more so, than sourcing via local crowd.

CONCLUSION

For nearly 70 years, intellectual access to our Islamic manuscripts collection was limited to a card-format handlist tucked away in the rare book room and occasional publications on the collection or specific manuscripts. With the completion of this project—iterative, collaborative, and leveraging the digital to afford scholarly engagement—we have not only realized enhanced intellectual access to the entire collection via richly detailed searchable descriptions and digital surrogates, but we have also set the stage for ongoing scholarly engagement with the collection, sure to shed even further light on the manuscripts' contents and their significance.

To facilitate that future scholarly engagement, I have prepared research guides to assist with navigating the database of topical and codicological data we have created. I also continue to maintain the project website, where we welcome supplemental descriptive contributions (beyond the essential) and to document the ongoing interactions of scholars with the collection. In fact, since manuscripts addressed in this project have fuller descriptions that those addressed in earlier projects (the 20 percent of the collection that we did not include), the project website might offer a platform by which we could gather descriptive enhancements for those other manuscripts, almost all of which have already been digitized.

Further, and in the interest of better understanding how our users have been engaging with the collection in the course of the project and how we might improve our digital offerings, another library colleague and I are currently conducting a user study for our digitized Islamic manuscripts. At this point we can say confidently that researchers are reaching our manuscripts (images and data) through the project website, HathiTrust, and even external websites for online forums and listservs, and they in turn are pointing their colleagues to our manuscripts. Needless to say, use and interest in the collection increased exponentially in the course of the project, and we cannot help but look forward to the future.

Evyn Kropf *is librarian for Near Eastern and Religious Studies and curator, Islamic Manuscripts Collection at the University of Michigan Library.*

NOTES

1. Crowdsourcing projects are now rampant in library circles, with mixed results that depend a great deal on interpretation in light of project aims. See Rose Holley, "Crowdsourcing: How and Why Should Libraries Do It?," *D-Lib Magazine* 16, no. 3/4 (2010); Christine Madsen, "Will 2011 Be the Year of Crowdsourcing in Libraries?" December 30, 2011, http://christinemadsen.com/2011/will-2012-be-the-year-of-crowdsourcing-in-libraries/; Johan Oomen and Lora Aroyo, "Crowdsourcing in the Cultural Heritage Domain: Opportunities and Challenges," in *Proceedings of the 5th International Conference on Communities and Technologies, Brisbane, QLD, Australia, June 29–July 02* (New York: ACM, 2011): 138–49; Ben Brumfield, "Lessons from Small Crowdsourcing Projects" talk at IMLS WebWise 2012 (transcribed in a blog post dated April 17, 2012, "Crowdsourcing at IMLS WebWise 2012," http://manuscripttranscription.blogspot.com/2012/03/crowdsourcing-at-imls-webwise-2012.html) and a series of recent blog posts by Trevor Owens (www.trevorowens.org/tag/crowdsourcing/).

2. Together these volumes, rolls, and leaves carry more than 1,800 titles. For more detail on the collection size, scope, history, and organization, see "About the Collection" on the collection research guide; Evyn Kropf, "Islamic Manuscripts Collection," http://guides.lib.umich.edu/islamicmss.

3. More on the grant program, selection criteria, funded projects, etc. may be found at "Cataloging Hidden Special Collections and Archives. About the Program," 2012, accessed June 1, 2013, www.clir.org/hiddencollections/index.html.

4. Created as a supplement to the second edition of the Anglo American Cataloging Rules (AACR2). See Gregory Pass, *Descriptive Cataloging of Ancient, Medieval, Renaissance, and Early Modern Manuscripts* (Chicago: Association of College and Research Libraries, 2003).

5. For details on the rationale behind these decisions, including selection of repository for the descriptive data and digital surrogates, see Evyn Kropf, "Within the Library Catalog and Beyond: Islamic Manuscripts at Michigan," forthcoming in the COMSt Handbook, "Chapter 3—Cataloguing."

6. For more on the original project concept and early implementation, see Evyn Kropf and Jonathan Rodgers, "Collaboration in Cataloguing: Islamic Manuscripts at Michigan," *MELA Notes*, no. 82 (2009): 17–29.

7. See Jan Just Witkam, "Aims and Methods of Cataloguing Manuscripts of the Middle East," in *Les manuscrits du Moyen-Orient: essais de codicologie et paléographie. Actes du Colloque d'Istanbul (Istanbul, 26–29 mai 1986)*, ed. François Déroche (Paris: Institut français d'études anatoliennes et Bibliothèque Nationale, 1989): 1–5; Annie Berthier and Marie Geneviève Guesdon, "Codicology and the History of Collections," in *Islamic Codicology: An Introduction to the Study of Manuscripts in Arabic Script*, ed. François Déroche et al. (London: Al-Furqān Islamic Heritage Foundation, 2006): 345–60; and Adam Gacek, "Appendix V. Describing the Manuscript," in *Arabic Manuscripts: A Vademecum for Readers* (Leiden: Brill, 2009): 333–38. The work completed at Princeton University Library for many of their Islamic manuscripts was also an inspiration.

8. These elements would characterize not only the contents of the codices (text, paratext, image, and ornament) through transcription, notes, and headings but also their form via further notes addressing the script and hand, structure (composition of gatherings, sewing, and cover), dimensions, writing surface, layout, and other physical aspects.

9. For more on the project website, see Kropf, "Within the Online Library Catalogue and Beyond: Islamic Manuscripts at Michigan"; Kropf and Rodgers, "Collaboration in Cataloguing," 2009.

10. As expected given the typical power distribution seen in small crowdsourcing projects; see Brumfield, "Lessons from Small Crowdsourcing Projects."

11. See this collection at http://babel.hathitrust.org/cgi/mb?a=listis;c=1961411403.

12. Rachel Stone's term; see "What Can the Vulgus Do?," August 17, 2010, http://magistraetmater.blog.co.uk/2010/08/17/what-can-the-vulgus-do-crowd-sourcing-for-medievalists-9195007/.

13. Due likely to the limited linguistic scope of our appeals and lack of established connections within the Islamic manuscript studies community at the opening of the project, we received enthusiastic response from our colleagues in Iran only rather late in the project.

EIGHT

Where There's a Will There's a Way

Using LibGuides to Rescue Paper Ephemera from the Bibliographic Underbrush

Sharon Farnel, Robert Cole, Robert Desmarais, Spencer Holizki, and Jeff Papineau, University of Alberta

Much has been written about the myriad ways that special collections libraries and archives can process collections with limited staffing, diminished opportunities for grants, obstacles to collaboration, and so on, but the detailed accounts from this literature do not always lay a practical foundation for the library and archival professions to resolve their particular challenges to make collections available quickly and efficiently. Too often, special collections librarians and archivists find themselves in the position of relegating newly acquired collections to the back of a long processing queue that may stretch back several years or perhaps decades. The authors of this case study, each with a vested interest and role in the project, describe how a challenging special collection was processed and outline how they developed a successful workflow to make the collection available in relatively short order to a large user base through streamlined processing to create an online finding aid using a tool available to many repositories, LibGuides.

The University of Alberta's Bruce Peel Special Collections Library has a long-established mandate to collect a wide range of printed, photographic, and manuscript material about the social, economic, and cultural development of the Canadian Prairie Provinces: Alberta, Saskatchewan, and Manitoba. What we now know as the Prairie Provinces Collection, a substantial and discrete collection within the University of Alberta Libraries, began with the bibliographic detective work and collection development of Bruce Braden Peel (1916–1998), who was chief librarian of the University of Alberta from 1955 to 1982. Peel recognized that the three provinces that comprise the Canadian Prairies are bound by social, economic, and cultural history into a single region, and he understood that its printed heritage would make it an ideal region to study. He began collecting this printed heritage for the library as well as documenting the early settlement and publishing history of western Canada in what is now considered the definitive bibliography of Canada's western interior, *A Bibliography of the Prairie Provinces to 1953*, first published in 1956 and twice revised and expanded. The Prairie Provinces Collection continues to grow today, not only as a physical collection but also as a digital library called Peel's Prairie Provinces (http://peel.library.ualberta.ca/), whose goal is to provide digital surrogates for as much of the physical collection as possible.

The Prairie Provinces Collection consists of several thousand printed volumes, as well as maps, photographs, and manuscripts housed in multiple locations on and off campus, including the Special Collections Library, the BARD (Book and Record Depository), and the Humanities and Social Sciences Library. And while most of the bound volumes in the collection are available to students, staff, and the general public as circulating books, other, more ephemeral materials—because of their value, fragility, special format, rarity, or a combination of these traits—are designated "noncirculating" and can only be accessed in the Special Collections Library's supervised reading room. A subcollection within the Prairie Provinces Collection, the diverse Prairie Ephemera Collection, includes posters, playbills, pamphlets, foldout maps, photographs, letters, menus, performance programs, clippings, brochures, flyers, advertisements, menus, railroad timetables, stock certificates, signs, typescripts, calendars, greeting cards, business documents, junk mail, political propaganda, forms, leaflets, tickets, and so on. These primary sources are a rich treasure trove of research material about the Canadian Prairies, providing invaluable historic testimony to the people and events that are underrepresented in traditional books. These prairie-themed acquisitions are commonly described locally as "Peelable" because they meet the basic criteria for being added to the collection; that is, they are printed or produced in the Canadian Prairies and/or they document the rich heritage of the Prairies.

Bruce Peel's diligent efforts to document and collect the paper records of the human experience in a vast Canadian region are carried on today by the Peel bibliographer and Special Collections librarian who regularly acquire new items for the Prairie Ephemera Collection through purchase or donation. Many new acquisitions are printed and bound like traditional books (e.g., yearbooks, cookbooks, telephone directories, genealogies), which are relatively simple to process because they are routed to Bibliographic Services for full cataloging treatment, including making their descriptions available in our online catalog, and the materials are then distributed to the appropriate library. Others, though not necessarily printed and bound like books, had to be processed in a more traditional way because they required a local note in the catalog record, either to recognize a major donor or to mark a special occasion (such as presentation to an honorary degree recipient). The remainder of the ephemera collection had been building up for several years under the leadership of a new Special Collections librarian who began acquiring a larger volume of ephemeral material for the library than had been done in the past, when only the most scarce and valuable printed ephemera were accepted for permanent inclusion in the collection.

While our collecting had expanded, there were, however, no practical means for us to process the growing collection beyond documenting basic information for purposes of inventory control. There were several reasons for our inertia. For one, printed and handwritten ephemera cannot be cataloged easily with item-level MARC records in the library's online catalog; such an approach would be impractical because traditional cataloging rules are difficult to apply (e.g., most items lack title pages and other bibliographic features that facilitate full cataloging treatment) and are not necessarily well suited to describing and organizing ephemera, "nontraditional" library items, and small collections of items (e.g., a stack of fur trade documents acquired as a set from a single donor). In addition, because the collection had remained largely uncataloged, no formal policy for organizing or describing these materials had yet been developed. Last, in the absence of a full-time archivist and with other library staff fully occupied with higher priority collections and services, the human resources to deal with the material were not available.

So our boxes of ephemera continued to pile up and multiply but we had no efficient way to make the contents more easily accessible for staff and discoverable at all by the outside world. We recognized that we had a rich, wonderful collection that had been essentially hidden from the world for too long, and we decided that something had to be done to make the collection available to researchers. We assembled a cross-disciplinary team comprised of the Special Collections librarian, Peel bibliographer, metadata librarian, library assistant, and a student from the School of Library and Information Studies, and set to work on a creative solution to make the collection available—not with individual cataloging records but with an archival finding aid with metadata robust enough to enable user discovery.

PLANNING

The team first identified the requirements of the project. We needed to define an approach for description that would address the following factors:

- When the ephemera materials were either donated or purchased, they had not been formally accessioned into the collection and assigned unique identifiers, which are essential to managing not only the physical objects but their descriptions as well.
- We needed to create descriptive metadata for all the materials in the backlog robust enough to ensure discoverability of the items by users in an online system.
- The entire collection would be digitized, as resources permit, and when digital surrogates are available, they would be added to the Peel's Prairie Provinces digital library; this project then needed to include item-level metadata that could also easily be converted into the MODS (Metadata Object Description Schema) format to accompany the images.
- The descriptions needed to be entered and made available via a discovery tool that was both easy to maintain and easy to use.
- We needed to do all of this with tools already used by the library; no additional funds could be spent to acquire new software.
- The work would need to be done by part-time student staff (who turn over regularly) and so it had to require minimal training or expertise.

It was actually an advantage that we had no legacy cataloging or previous policy for organizing and describing these materials, since that gave us a free hand in creating our new policies. In addition, although the materials share the core characteristic of relating to the Canadian Prairies, they do not constitute an archival fond in the traditional sense, which also gave us flexibility in how to approach them. For these reasons, we felt free to use any strategy for arranging and describing the materials, as long as it met our requirements. During initial project meetings, the team laid out and discussed four possible approaches, each of which had advantages and disadvantages in terms of the parameters outlined above.

The first approach discussed was to fold the processing and description of these materials into those already established for the Peel's Prairie Provinces digital library and to create individual MODS descriptions for ephemera objects. This approach naturally offered several advantages. First, established guidelines and tools for metadata creation specific to the digital library could be used, which would not only promote consistency in metadata format and content but also mean that the metadata was already in the MODS format. Second, the descriptions would be immediately available for browsing and searching within the Peel's Prairie Provinces digital library. However, this approach also presented several disadvantages. From a very pragmatic point of view, user account creation and maintenance for the database supporting the digital library is somewhat involved. In addition, training on the metadata creation tool and the standard used (MODS) would be quite labor intensive. Moreover, with the existing Peel's Prairie Provinces digital library, we have attempted as much as possible to have digital surrogates for described items, and so there was a concern about adding a substantial number of descriptions for items that are not yet available digitally.

The second approach was to describe the collection as a whole, creating a stand-alone finding aid (encoded in HTML) that could be housed on one of the libraries' servers along with a handful of finding aids that have been created in the past. Advantages of this approach would be that an existing template, based on Rules for Archival Description (RAD) and developed several years ago by a practicum student, could be copied and followed, which might make training on the descriptive aspect of the work somewhat simpler and quicker. And because there is a precedent for these types of items within the system, adding one additional finding aid would not be problematic. One disadvantage of this approach was that training on HTML encoding would be required, as would the licensing and installation of HTML editing software on workstations. Secondly, access to these pages items is through IT staff only, and so updating and revising them is a somewhat involved process. While this works well for items that will not change, for those that will be revised and enhanced on a regular basis, such as the finding aid for this collection, the processes become overly cumbersome. Most importantly, this approach would not result in item-level descriptions, which will be necessary for eventual inclusion of the materials in the Peel's Prairie Provinces digital library and that might be more helpful to users of this kind of collection, which is not a traditional archival fond.

The third option discussed was to use Archivists' Toolkit, which is being used for a large, more traditional archival fond housed within the libraries. Advantages of this approach were that the tool is custom-designed for describing archival collections and, because it is already in use within the system, expertise in its use and support is available to draw on. An additional advantage is that it allows for export of metadata in a variety of formats, including the format (MODS) that will be needed when these items are incorporated into the Peel's Prairie Provinces digital library. However, this approach also offered several fairly significant disadvantages. The first was that user account setup and maintenance is much more labor intensive, and use requires installation of software on individual workstations. In addition, fairly extensive training on the tool and description would be required, which would place an unreasonable demand on an already overburdened part-time archivist if she were required to offer the toolkit training to a succession of library school students. Last, the toolkit does not come with a built-in method for displaying item descriptions or full finding aids online, and so the problem of where to house and make this finding aid accessible would still be outstanding.

The final approach was to develop some basic guidelines for describing individual items and to house these descriptions in a finding aid using the LibGuides software. LibGuides (http://springshare.com/libguides/) is a popular content management system for creating and sharing research and subject guides. This approach offered several advantages. First, the libraries had an existing LibGuides account and so support and expertise was available to draw on when needed. Second, the tab and subtab structure of LibGuides lends itself well to creating categories and subcategories of items, and structuring the content in the form of tables allows for easy export and conversion to other formats (e.g., XML). Third, the software is very easy to learn and work with, does not require installation on local workstations, and is very straightforward in terms of user account creation and maintenance. And finally, the finding aid would be immediately available on the libraries' website, the structure navigable, and the content fully searchable. The main disadvantages of this approach were that the LibGuides software was not necessarily designed for this purpose and so might not lend itself perfectly to the type of content at hand. Furthermore, there was some concern about the level of navigability and searchability available within the LibGuides software, and how well it would scale as the collection continued to grow from hundreds of items to tens of thousands.

In the end, the team decided to pursue the last approach: developing descriptions in a LibGuides finding aid. Although item-level descriptions would not be found by searching the libraries' catalog, researchers would ultimately find those descriptions when they discovered the guide. And the guide itself would be easily discoverable because it would have a collection-level record in the catalog and would be indexed on the libraries' website and by Google. We felt that this strategy would allow us to get descriptions of the materials online and make them searchable quickly with few technical or training hurdles. This would give us the best results given the resources—human, financial, and technical—that we had available.

IMPLEMENTATION

Once the team agreed on the desired approach, the project really required very little to get it off the ground. First, we created a basic accession template from an existing Special Collections accession register. The template included 13 elements for capturing key information: title, inclusive dates (approximate), description/condition, barcode/accession number, creator, collection, donor/dealer name, value, date received, date accessioned/processed, location (of original items), digitized (yes or no), and (in) LibGuide (yes or no). A set of folders was created on a shared network drive so that staff in both Bibliographic Services and Special Collections would have access to all the forms. The accession template, completed accession documents, as well as project guidelines and other documents would be kept in this shared area. A separate series of barcodes (beginning with PE for "Prairie Ephemera") was ordered for use with these materials. This allows for a unique identifier to be applied to each item using a series of numbers patterned after those for our other digitized Prairie materials (e.g., PC for postcard).

Because there is not enough space to accommodate students working on the project in Special Collections, a secure procedure for moving materials back and forth between Special Collections and Bibliographic Services was agreed upon, and a process was initiated for sharing archival supplies (e.g., Mylar sleeves, acid-free envelopes) between the two units. Although this requires somewhat greater effort to coordinate movement of materials and supplies, it is outweighed by the fact that the students are closer to the Peel bibliographer and metadata librarian, the two main resources for training and consultation, who have their offices in the Bibliographic Services space. Staff in the Special Collections Library prioritize the materials to be processed and ensure that there is space for housing the items in barcode number order once they are returned fully processed and described.

Prior to starting work on individual items, the finding aid structure had to be created in LibGuides (see http://guides.library.ualberta.ca/prairieephemera). Based on an assessment of the materials to be accessioned and described first, as well as on a general sense of the most common types of materials in the collection, the basic structure of the finding aid, as reflected in the tabs, was created. We decided to organize the materials into broad categories, grouped under LibGuides' genre tabs. One group of broad categories was based on the physical format of ephemera items (e.g., photographic prints or letters), but we also included broad categories based on the purpose of the materials (e.g., business or personal correspondence) or broader topics (e.g., religion, education, advertisements). The initial category tabs created were Photographs, Memoirs, Letters, and Posters. A basic description of the collection as a whole was added to the Home tab, and within the others the table structure was put in place. A collection-level record, with a pointer to the finding aid, was created in the local catalog, to be unshadowed (i.e., made public) once some content had been added.

In developing a format for the students to use in describing the individual items, we decided not to attempt any kind of encoded description, which is also more in keeping with the free text usually used in LibGuides. The decision to use tables allows us to keep the amount of information provided for each item brief but descriptive, and provides a basic underlying structure that will make later conversion of the metadata easier. Additionally, because the work was to be done exclusively by students and because we wanted to see it move along as quickly as possible, a short-form model for description was developed that would provide users with pertinent information while not requiring reliance on AACR2 or Rules for Archival Description (RAD) formalities. The descriptive guidelines are a simplified version of those used for materials in the Peel's Prairie Provinces digital library, which in turn are based on the guidelines used by Bruce Peel in compiling his seminal bibliography of the Canadian prairies. (Mr. Peel was both a librarian and a trained bibliographer, and so his guidelines combine the traditions of descriptive bibliography and library cataloging.)

For the sake of readability and brevity, item descriptions were separated into three required elements: unique identifier (Prairie Ephemera barcode number), date or date range, and a consistently structured sentence-type description that makes mention of the relevant elements of each item to be described, including a reference to the item type, its physical condition, its content, authors or names associated, and a location, for example: "PE000736 | 1907 | 8"x10" B&W print, mounted, showing several horse teams and work crews in Calgary." The idea behind this method of description was to allow for separation and organization of items based on date or unique identifier, and for item descriptions to be more easily broken down at a later date into appropriate fields of metadata based on the syntactic structure of the descriptive sentence. We also decided to use the date to determine the order in which descriptions appear. As new descriptions are added, the items are automatically listed in chronological order under the appropriate tab.

In describing the items, each brief narrative draws its vocabulary from Library of Congress Subject Headings (LCSH), Library of Congress Thesaurus for Graphic Materials (TGM), and Canadian Subject Headings (CSH). That is, each item is not provided with subject headings, but the vocabulary for its description is based on the vocabularies from whence subject headings could be derived. Under ideal circumstances, separate subject or genre headings would be included in descriptions of such materials. However, we decided not to have the students assign subject or genre headings to ephemera items at this stage because of the extensive training it would require. The lack of such headings is mitigated to some degree by the prose descriptions of the items, which are completely full-text searchable, as well as by the broad subject categorization provided by the tab structure (see figure 8.1).

Our goal to have the project move quickly and with little demand for additional resources was successful. The total time commitment from staff from both Bibliographic Services and the Special Collections Library, including initial project discussions and planning, preparation of docu-

Advertisements and Promotional Material

Accession No.	Date	Title & Description
PE000578	Feb.? 1902	Small, bound notebook with graph paper and a red cover, advertising for the Great-West Life Assurance Co. Front inside cover, centrefold and back cover of the book are stamped with statistics about the company. There are a few handwritten notes inside, including two short love poems.
PE000654	[1905?]	Bookmark advertising for the Canadian Northern Railway's Short Line which ended in Edmonton, Alberta. Includes a list of ticket agent's names who offered Homeseekers' rates.
PE000238	1907	Small calendar courtesy of J.H. Morris & Co. dept. store, features colour print of portrait painting by Rudolf Weisse, Edmonton, Alberta.
PE004942	1912	10"x14" poster showing the bar room of the Selkirk Hotel. Poster is rolled into a scroll, slightly flattened in the centre, but otherwise in good condition.
PE000683	Feb. 5, 1912	Train schedule for the Soo-Spokane Route run by the Spokane International Railway. Centrefold is a map of the route which runs from Portland, Oregon up through Calgary, Alberta and Moose Jaw, Saskatchewan and down to St. Paul, Minnesota. Includes time schedules of the international route and of connecting train lines, as well as a description of the trains and equipment in use.
PE000401	1913	Poster with tear-away calendar and image of horse. Each month on the calendar is intact, with staples for added support. The entire item is a promotional calendar for the Battleford Horse Exchange, whose proprietor is A.M. Speers.
PE000646	[1913]	Two handbills promoting immigration to Western Canada: Mirror, Alta., Moose Jaw, Sask., Rosetown, Sask., and Port Alberni, B.C.
PE000884	ca. 1914?	Scrip coupon issued by Arcade Confectionery, Calgary, Alberta. The coupon owner is due a ½ mile of first class travel on any steam ship or steam railway in the world. Features two delicate line drawings of a steam train and a steam ship.
PE000392	ca. 1918	Poster advertising the closing out sale of the Baldwin Department Store in Cabri, Saskatchewan. This item appears to have been advertised in or printed by the Clarion.
PE000709	1918-1919	9"x6" catalogue of supplies for vets, breeders, and stockmen from the Winnipeg Veterinary and Breeders Supply Company. Catalogue is in good condition.
PE004935	1920-1926	8"x11" booklet entitled "Plans for the Home Builder: obtainable from your hometown lumber dealer." In decent condition; slight water discolouration on back cover and edges of pages.

Figure 8.1. Sample item descriptions from the Advertisements and Promotional Material category.

mentation, initial creation of the base LibGuides finding aid, selection and prioritization of materials for processing and description, and student training amounted to no more than 15 hours. In the summer of 2011, we created user accounts in LibGuides for our student worker and conducted some basic training on the use of the LibGuides software. Staff in Special Collections (including the part-time conservator) demonstrated the basic techniques for proper archival housing, and the metadata librarian and Peel bibliographer conducted some training on application of the descriptive guidelines.

We began with one student working on the project. The student was going into the second year of the MLIS program at the School of Library and Information Studies at the University of Alberta, with which the libraries are, naturally, closely affiliated. He had completed courses in cataloging and information organization and had just completed a practicum at a military archive. His background in history and an interest in the ephemeral record were also beneficial as he undertook this work.

Staff in Special Collections prioritized materials for processing and description, and worked with the student to ensure a continuous flow of materials to Bibliographic Services as the workflow demanded. The student would work on materials in the order in which they arrived. The ephemera items come arranged according to "accession," which, in the context of this project, simply reflected items that were purchased or donated as a discrete set. Accessions varied in size from a single item to many and in the degree to which they were a coherent set; some contained items of a similar format, other items related to a particular event, others had no obvious logical relationship beyond the Prairie theme. Each accession would include a very basic, handwritten inventory document that would have been created by Special Collections at the time of donation/purchase. If any necessary information was missing, the student noted this as such in the accession document being created for the project. The student would assign a unique identifier (i.e., barcode number) to each item in the accession and enter this along with the descriptive information, formulated according to the guidelines, into the accession document.

In creating the description for the item, the student would refer to the appropriate vocabularies and authority lists for guidance. If necessary, some additional online research could be conducted, though the student was advised to keep the time spent to a reasonable level. Once the information was complete, the student transferred the necessary pieces—barcode number, date/date range, and description—to the appropriate tab in the LibGuides finding aid, making it immediately visible to the public. In cases where an item might easily be placed in more than one category, the student was given leeway to determine which tab was the most appropriate. The Peel bibliographer and metadata librarian were also consulted as needed. The accession document was marked with the status of "in LibGuides," saved with an appropriate filename (following the pattern of "item type, date accessioned"; e.g., "Three letters, July 15, 2011"), and moved into a separate folder on the shared drive space so that it was clear that the accession was complete. The Peel bibliographer and metadata librarian reviewed the descriptions on a regular basis in case there were questions or concerns.

In this process, the student worked more or less independently, requiring minimal oversight from staff. Our ongoing work with students on the project, including training, consultation on description, and moving of materials to and from Special Collections, amounts to no more than a few hours every two weeks or so.

Completed descriptions are displayed using tables in the LibGuides software. An early concern was the potential need for scrolling that would be required for those categories, such as Photographs, with large numbers of items. Initially this was handled by creating anchors at the top of a tab that were linked to sections further down the tab. For example, the phrase "1900–1909," when clicked on, would jump the user down to the point in the table where the list of items dated from 1900 to 1909 began. Although this worked initially, we recently discovered that there is a character limit on tabs imposed by the LibGuides software, and so we have developed and implemented a different system for handling the categories with greater numbers of items, such as photographs. We have started using subtabs to separate items by date range. For example, the Photographs tab now includes subtabs for Pre-1900, 1900–1909, and so on, and on the main tab itself there are links to each of the subtabs (see figure 8.2).

Although our process generally worked smoothly, one early challenge was to develop a system for numbering items. As mentioned earlier, the materials as received from Special Collections were organized simply by date of donation or purchase. In some cases, purchases of items (e.g., a set of photographs or letters) were more akin to a discrete collection than simple miscellanea and were more appropriately accessioned in that manner. Other cases were not as clear, as materials were not always grouped according to a specific characteristic (e.g., date of creation, genre, subject, etc.). It was initially thought that these groupings should be retained as the basis of the accession, and work has continued under this assumption. However, we recognize that this may not be the ideal method for accessioning and have been discussing possibilities for organizing the accessions differently.

Another challenge we face is the lack of a sophisticated system for tracking accessions. Because accession documents are stored as individual Microsoft Word files, and the files are located on a shared drive rather than in a content management system (CMS) or database, retrieval of accession information for individual items can be time consuming and slightly cumbersome. Character limits for file names prevent the naming of accession files with much more than the basic item type and date of accession, although naming them with barcode ranges is an option that we are considering. In addition, we are planning to examine the folder structure in our shared drive space to determine ways of making it more flexible.

RESULTS

Planning for the project got under way in the summer of 2011 and work began in earnest within a few weeks. To date, nearly 800 items have been

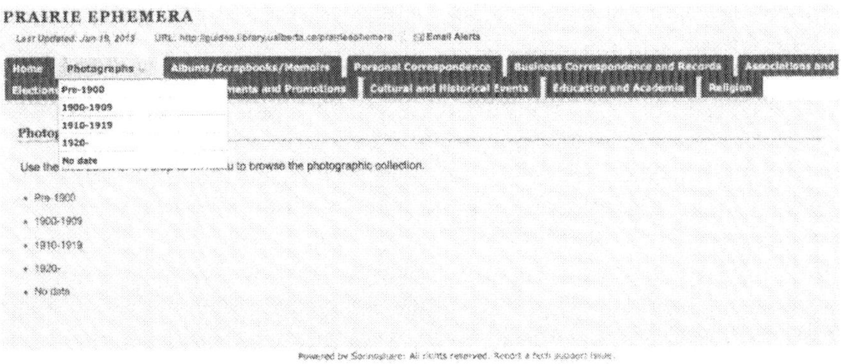

Figure 8.2. Date range sub-tabs from the Photographs category.

accessioned and described. Due to demand from other high-priority projects, we are only able to have one student working on the project at any given time, and only for a portion of their total work hours. Normally, during the summers this amounts to 12–15 hours per week, during the term 3–5 hours per week. We are quite pleased with the amount and quality of the work completed to date given the amount of time invested.

Overall, we feel that the solution chosen has quite successfully met the requirements we identified for the project. Each of the items now has a unique identifier (barcode number) that ties it to an accession document as well as a basic description. We now have item-level descriptions that are sufficient for discovery in an online system, and we have a basic structure that will make later metadata conversion simpler. The system chosen, LibGuides, allows for searching and browsing of the content, which adds to discoverability, and is also very easy to use and maintain. There was no additional cost for license or purchase of the software, and internal expertise was available to draw on. The processes and procedures are fairly straightforward, the students who have worked on the project have been able to start producing quality results very quickly, and the draw on other staff time has been minimal.

The Prairie Ephemera project has been extremely well received by the various constituencies involved in its planning and implementation. For library administration, the system has facilitated the relatively rapid and cost-efficient accessioning of a valuable set of material that would otherwise have remained invisible to researchers. For library staff, the Prairie Ephemera finding aid has provided an effective and responsive way to inventory, organize, and access a wide array of material. The finding aid has been used to respond to requests as varied and unique as the items contained in the collection. For example, we have used it to find material by format such as examples of photographic/reprographic processes for art history students (e.g., stereoscope cards, gelatin prints). We've used it for the selection of material by content (e.g., request for manuscript material related to the Canadian fur trade for a digitization project initiated by a third-party vendor), as well as for selection of material by type (e.g., request for Prairie Chinese food restaurant menus for inclusion in an exhibition at the Royal Alberta Museum). It has also been very helpful in responding to internal requests to verify holdings to avoid duplication when purchasing material for the Prairie Provinces Collection.

In fact, because of the general success of the model, we have already applied it to a large set of sexual-health and disease-prevention pamphlets dating from the early days of the AIDS/HIV crisis (http://guides.library.ualberta.ca/hivaids). In addition, the Clennell Dickins Collection—a largely photographic and more traditional archival fond related to the history of aviation in western Canada—has also been processed in this manner and will be made publicly available shortly. And as other collections come to be handled, we will certainly consider this model as a very strong contender.

The students who have been recruited to work on these projects, who have generally been those in library science or library technician programs, have also been universally favorable in their reflections on their time working with the Prairie Ephemera Collection. Such enthusiasm is, of course, partially grounded in pragmatic considerations; students naturally cherish paid employment, especially when it is professionally related. The Prairie Ephemera project, however, has been perceived as offering particularly valuable vocational training for young librarians and archivists. Certainly students involved in the accessioning of Peel items are involved with every facet of the process from description to physical preparation and storage. The result is a work experience that allows students to gain firsthand knowledge across the gamut of the collection-management cycle and refine a wide range of skills learned in organization of knowledge and archives coursework. Perhaps even more importantly, they are granted considerable license to exercise their professional judgment. Given the eclectic nature of the Prairie Ephemera Collection, the students accessioning these artifacts are inevitably faced with numerous instances where they must adapt project guidelines to anomalous circumstances.

Based on the project's limited interaction with researchers as well as preliminary investigation of usage statistics, external users also appear to be pleased with the Prairie Ephemera Collection. Staff in the Special Collections Library filled a handful of requests from users who have contacted them regarding an item they discovered in the finding aid. Basic statistics collected as part of the LibGuides software indicates that in the six months of 2011 that the finding aid was live, it received nearly 500 total page views. In 2012, the number grew to just over 1,400, and 2013 (January to July) has seen more than 800. It seems that Photographs and Albums/Scrapbooks/Memoirs are the most popular categories.

LESSONS LEARNED

Overall, the processing of the Prairie Ephemera Collection has been extremely successful, serving for us as a prototype for the handling of other collections that are not amenable to traditional cataloging practices and certainly providing a model worthy of consideration by other institutions. Having said that, there is no such thing as a perfect system or process, and so we have had to make some changes along the way and have others yet to contemplate.

With regard to the management side of things, we will be examining the naming convention we use for the accession documents as well as the folder structure we use on the shared drive space in hopes that we might make finding and accessing details for specific items simpler for internal staff purposes.

We have also begun thinking about alternate ways in which to organize the accessions. As has already been described, the accessions are currently defined by the way in which the materials come to us from Special Collections. However, in many cases these groupings often have no defining characteristic beyond a specific date of donation or purchase, and as such are not traditional archival fonds. In these cases, we feel there is less of a need to keep these materials together as accessions and so we are open to other means of organization.

As has been noted, we have found that there are certain technical limits imposed by the software, which we have to work around. For example, we described how we discovered a character limit for the tabs and the way in which we began using subtabs as a means of getting around that. There may yet be other technical barriers that we run up against, and when we do we will have to put our heads together and come up with a solution.

Last, as we have worked through the collection we have found that our initial set of categories (as reflected in the names of the tabs) was neither extensive nor specific enough to capture the nuances of the materials. We started with four tabs (Photographs, Memoirs, Letters, and Posters), but as of July 2013 we now have ten: Photographs, Albums/Scrapbooks/Memoirs, Personal Correspondence, Business Correspondence and Records, Associations and Unions, Elections and Government, Advertisements and Promotions, Cultural and Historical Events, Education and Academia, and Religion. We fully appreciate that this categorization must be flexible as we are dealing with a large and growing collection, which has quite porous boundaries.

CONCLUSION

As we move forward, we plan to continue accessioning Prairie Ephemera materials, both those in the backlog and those newly acquired, according to the model developed. In addition, we plan to examine some of the more ephemera-like materials (e.g., local theater programs, serial advertisements) currently in the queue for handling via the regular Peel's Prairie Provinces digital library route, to determine whether or not they might better be handled as part of the Prairie Ephemera Collection proper or through a similar process into individual, theme-based finding aids.

In addition, when digitization of these materials becomes imminent, we will have to think about the relationship between the Prairie Ephemera Collection and its finding aid and the Peel's Prairie Provinces digital library. Where will the metadata and digital surrogates "live"—in the finding aid as well as in the digital library? Will a decision be made to do away with the finding aid and incorporate everything, including metadata for nondigitized objects, into the digital library? These questions will require careful attention and examination of existing policies, procedures, and workflows. Although this is a discussion for some time in the future, it is an important one and must be carefully engaged and thoughtfully handled.

With regard to the LibGuides software, we will continue to examine both existing and new functionalities to determine which, if any, might enhance the usability of the finding aid and assist in promoting the collection. Options we will consider are using the social media widgets or tagging and commenting functionality (so users might submit valuable metadata, such as identifying a relative in a photo). As well, as the collection continues to grow, we will monitor the LibGuides software for any technical challenges that may arise (e.g., limits to amount of content in a tab, or need for navigational aids for tabs with large amounts of content). We will need to outline potential options should these challenges become insurmountable.

A major task ahead is systematic assessment of the usage and usability of the finding aid. The LibGuides software captures quite extensive statistics on usage which, when combined with information drawn from our instance of Google Analytics, should give us some valuable insights into usage. In addition, we plan to work with the University of Alberta's assessment librarian to conduct a more systematic evaluation of user opinion and habits to help us understand how well the descriptions meet user needs. The results of these two avenues of investigation will inform decisions around the way in which the collection is organized and described, potential revisions to functionality, and means of promotion of the collection.

The University of Alberta Libraries is certainly not alone in facing the challenge of bringing to light "hidden" collections and in doing so with minimal resources to spare. We feel that we have developed a process that allows us to work through our Prairie Ephemera materials in an efficient way while still providing meaningful access for our users. And in doing so, we have demonstrated the ways in which a cross-disciplinary team can come together to find creative solutions that serve the needs of collections, users, and the organization.

Sharon Farnel *is metadata librarian,* ***Robert Cole*** *is Peel bibliographer,* ***Robert Desmarais*** *is special collections librarian,* ***Spencer Holizki*** *is librarian, and* ***Jeff Papineau*** *is library assistant at the University of Alberta.*

NINE

Describing Records, People, Organizations, and Functions

The Empowering the User Project's Flexible Archival Catalog

Clare Paterson, University of Glasgow

As archivists, we look to represent an archive's provenance and preserve its original order when using fonds-based arrangement and description. However, this can only represent one understanding of the creation and use of the archive. In applying a fonds-based approach, we always make compromises: Records are arranged to fit an administrative structure in place for some, but not all, of an organization's history, or a functional analysis provides an adequate structure, but one that, nevertheless, fails to reflect all the uses of a record across its lifecycle. For complex organizations the traditional, monohierarchical structure in which records are arranged and described simply cannot represent the multiple contexts and complex relationships in which records are created and used.

University of Glasgow Archive Services manages two significant collections: the University Archive and the Scottish Business Archive. Both collections include large archives that were created and maintained by complex organizations. In managing these archives, we have faced challenges in implementing traditional fonds-based arrangement and description. As archival theory developed to recognize the multiple contexts of the records continuum, we became aware of the failure of fonds-based descriptive practice to represent these multiple contexts.

To address this problem, we have investigated developing an approach to cataloging that provides what we think is a sounder and more objective basis for archival description than conventional hierarchical, fonds-based arrangement. We wanted to find a way of describing records in which there is no single structure into which the records must be forced. Our investigation has resulted in a methodology in which there are separate descriptions of the records and of the people, organizations, functions, and activities associated with their creation and use. Identifying and describing the relationships among these records, people, organizations, functions, and activities prompts consideration of the ways in which the records interacted, why they were created, and how they were used. Arguably this requires a closer analysis of the records and a deeper understanding of their creation and use than is required for traditional arrangement and description. This analysis and the resulting description of these components results in a more flexible approach to presenting the records and their context, which allows users the freedom to define for themselves how they want to approach understanding them.

This case study examines efforts at the University of Glasgow to explore new ways of representing these multiple contexts in our Empowering the User (EtU) project.[1] It looks at the development of the cataloging methodology, the identification of relevant international standards, the selection and modification of standards-compliant document-type definitions (DTDs) for the separate descriptive components (records, organizations and people, and functions and activities), and the development of an online interface that takes advantage of this new approach to describing both records and their context. The EtU project offers evidence there is considerable value in the exploration of different approaches to description, both in terms of determining the primary level of description and in considering how and what we describe.

PLANNING

In Archive Services, we first looked to explore a new approach to archival description through Developing Archival Context (DAC) Standards for Functions in the Higher Education Sector. DAC described the functions and activities of Scotland's Higher Education sector and incorporated these descriptions into the online catalog for the collections, Gateway to the Archives of Scottish Higher Education (GASHE). Descriptions of functions and activities include listings of the records created and used in their performance and of the administrative units involved in carrying out these functions.[2]

DAC established that these additional descriptive components enhanced the traditional catalog. However, the records themselves were still described within a static fonds-based arrangement that offered only one interpretation of each institution. A key recommendation of the project was further work to develop an approach to cataloging that separates descriptions of the context in which the records were created and used from the descriptions of the records themselves in order to represent all the appropriate contexts in which the records were maintained. Having worked with higher education archives, we looked to the Scottish Business Archive for a suitable test-bed for our further development work. The House of Fraser Archive offered exceptional potential.

House of Fraser is one of Britain's largest department store retailers. It was founded in 1849 when Arthur & Fraser opened as a retail drapery on Glasgow's up-and-coming Argyle Street. Over the course of the 20th century, a period of expansion saw House of Fraser establish a presence in towns and cities the length and breadth of the United Kingdom. This expansion was powered by a run of acquisitions of other department stores, including, in 1959, the prestigious Harrods group. Comprising 130 linear meters of over 10,000 items dating from the early 19th century, the archive is a large collection. With the records of over 200 individual stores, many of which predate the foundation of House of Fraser itself, it is also a complex collection. This complexity has brought considerable challenges for the archivists who have sought to arrange and catalog it effectively. In the early 2000s, a recataloging project adopted a functional approach to arrangement and description, but it proved difficult to accurately reflect the contexts in which the records were created and used.

As DAC progressed and our ideas about a new approach to descriptive practice developed, we also considered the delivery of any resultant catalog online and the potential of information technology to enhance access. By the mid-2000s, a large number of retro conversion projects of paper-based finding aids and guides had been completed, delivering online catalogs. However, these projects primarily exploited technology to get existing catalogs available and searchable in the online world. In effect, they delivered keyword-searchable paper catalogs, rather than harnessing technology to develop new ways of delivering descriptions of archives. We were interested in the potential of new technologies for enhancing user access, particularly in offering multiple ways of discovering the information held within them.

To take forward the recommendations of DAC, Archive Services submitted a bid to the Arts and Humanities Research Council (AHRC) through the Resource Enhancement Scheme. Empowering the User: The Development of Flexible Archival Catalogues was designed to test the concept of catalogs that represent the multiple contexts and complex relationships of records and to deliver an online, flexible archive catalog for the House of Fraser Archive. The bid was successful, and from 2006 until 2009 the project team tested the application of a new approach to description on the archive resulting in an online catalog, launched in 2011 (see figure 9.1).[3]

The foundations of the new cataloging methodology we implemented in EtU were put in place through the recommendations of DAC.[4] DAC's main recommendation was to reject the monohierarchical representation of the context of an archive as traditionally implemented through fonds-based arrangement and description. In its place would be a method of description that separated descriptions of the contexts of the archive from descriptions of the content of the archive.

Separating records from their context removed the familiar pattern of description from fonds through to item, reflecting administrative structure or functional purpose. We therefore had to decide at what level to arrange and describe records. Describing records at the level of the series (as used successfully particularly in Australia) looked to be a useful model.[5] The record series is arguably the most natural aggregation of records. Series are often concrete entities; they can be readily identified and pointed to and, most importantly, are what people and organizations actually produce in the course of their work. Record series would, therefore, be our highest level of description.

The contexts of the archive would be represented through authority records. These would act as the main structure of the catalog and offer access routes to the records for users. Having chosen to place the authority record at the center of our new cataloging system, we had to define what these authority records would describe. Again, the foundations for the project came from our previous experience. Based on traditional practice, authority records for organizations creating the records would be

Figure 9.1. The House of Fraser online catalogue homepage.

included. We saw that this could be extended to include a description of every incarnation of an organization and each significant person involved in the creation and use of the records. In addition, building on the success of DAC, we also looked to test the value of including authority records for functions and activities as part of the contexts of the House of Fraser Archive.

At this stage, we had in place a plan with five different descriptive components: record series, people, organizations, functions, and activities. The next stage was to map out the ways in which these descriptive components would interact in order to reflect the multiple contexts of the records. Indeed, we realized that the value of our cataloging approach was found in the relationships between the descriptive components. In our methodology, an individual description by itself—whether of a record series, person, or function—would be of limited value to users. However, when linked to related descriptions, the full value of the records and the contexts in which they were maintained could be made explicit. A system of rules governing the interaction between and within the descriptive components was developed. We spent time mapping out the possible relationships between the descriptive components. With its clear outline of descriptive entities and their relationships, the map of entities for Archives Investigator, the New South Wales government online catalog, was particularly helpful.[6] We developed a similar map for describing the House of Fraser Archive (see figure 9.2).

Our planning also considered the way in which our catalog would be made available online. Our existing online catalog was not capable of managing the multiple descriptive components and the links between them. Similarly, it could not offer the user the flexibility in discovery we wanted to promote. We looked to our colleagues in the university's Humanities Advanced Technology and Information Institute (HATII) to develop a system that would deliver a flexible presentation of the catalog.

IMPLEMENTATION

An AHRC grant of £200,000 funded the three-year EtU applied research project. The majority of the funding was allocated to staff costs: a full-time research archivist for three years, with additional part-time staffing for the development of a retail-sector business function model and project management. Then, £10,000 was allocated to the development of the online catalog. The appropriate expertise for the project was found within Archive Services' staff, minimizing training requirements. Victoria Peters, research archivist on DAC, held the same position on EtU. Lesley Richmond, university archivist, was principal investigator. Rachel Hosker, assistant archivist (Business Collections) was responsible for the development of the retail-sector function model. Victoria was responsible

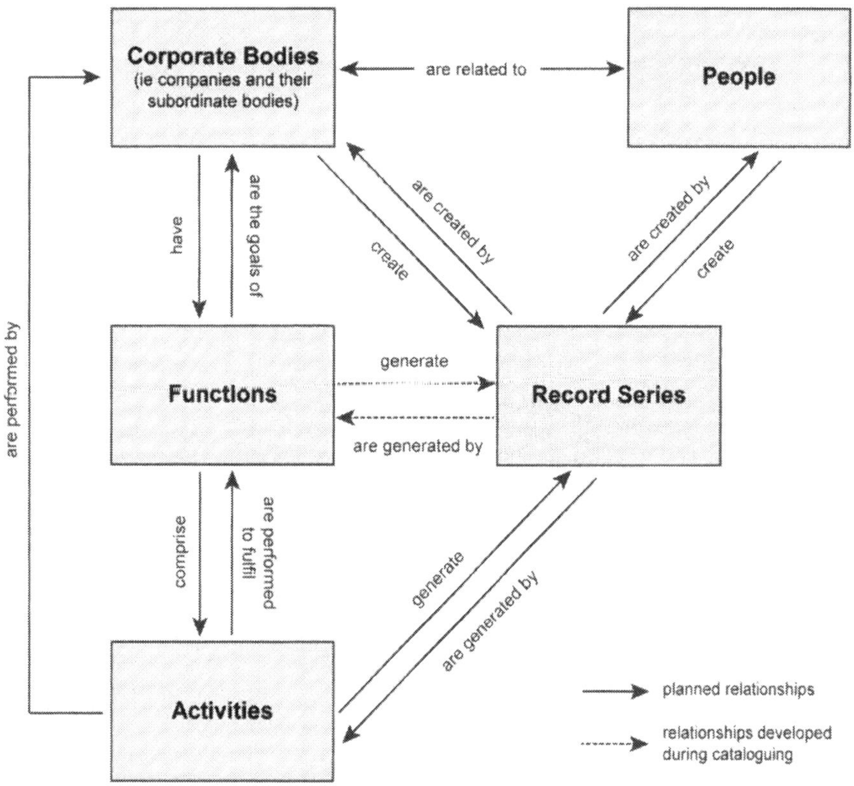

Figure 9.2. Map of relationships between descriptive components for the House of Fraser Archive.

for the development of the cataloging methodology, the creation of standards-compliant templates for the descriptive components, and for the cataloging of the House of Fraser Archive to test the methodology and its implementation. She also worked closely with HATII's consultant on the delivery of the online catalog.

Although moving away from fonds-based description, we did not wish to move away from international standards for description. So, record-series descriptions were created in line with General International Standard Archival Description [ISAD(G)], descriptions of people and organizations complied with the International Standard Archival Authority Record for Corporate Bodies, Persons and Families [ISAAR(CPF)], and the International Standard for Describing Functions (ISDF) was used for function and activity descriptions.[7]

With the appropriate content standards identified, we needed to determine how to structure our descriptions. Knowing that we would be delivering our descriptions as XML data, standards-compliant document-type definitions (DTDs) were used for each descriptive component. Our choice for the record-series descriptions was easy: Encoded Archival Description (EAD) provides a widely adopted, stable, and ISAD(G)-compliant DTD. Similarly, although Encoded Archival Context (EAC) was still only in a beta version, since it was ISAAR(CPF) compliant and developed by well-recognized archivists, it was quickly adopted as our DTD for the organization and people descriptive components.

For our remaining two types of authority records, functions and activities, there was not yet an associated XML encoding standard we could adopt. Using EAC as a model, an Encoded Archival Function (EAF) DTD was developed. EAC was suitable due to the close links between ISAAR(CPF) and ISDF. EAF simply borrows relevant elements of EAC and includes the four ISDF elements not found in ISAAR(CPF). These elements are: classification (ISDF: 5.1.5), description (ISDF: 5.2.2), legislation (ISDF: 5.2.4), and type (ISDF: 5.3.2).

With these decisions, the structure for the descriptions of records, companies, people, functions, and activities were achieved through the use of the standard XML DTDs (and the prototype EAF). However, because we were planning to describe archival materials in a new way, these DTDs did not include all the elements of description we required to represent the relationships between the records and their contexts. To overcome this, we developed project rules for the use of the elements available in each DTD to allow the relationships outlined in our map of descriptive components to be represented.

Specifically, for linking record series to the companies that created and used them, the "Name of Creator" [ISAD(G): 3.2.1] and <origination> (EAD) element looked to be perfectly suited. However, to comply with ISAD(G), this element should only be used to describe the creator of the series; the standard does not permit this element to be used for companies that contribute to or use records but do not create them. This type of relationship is not recognized within ISAD(G) or EAD. Therefore, we had to adopt a project rule that expanded the definition of this descriptive element to encompass all companies with an involvement in creating and using a particular record series. This was most commonly seen where one company succeeded another and retained the same series of records.

We also needed to link descriptions of record series to descriptions of the functions or activities which created the records. However, there is no element representing this type of relationship within ISAD (G) or EAD. Rather than creating a new element of description, we adapted the EAD element <controlaccess>. This, however, is intended for access points or index terms for a record, not as a link to a related descriptive component. This raised a particular problem as we were also using <controlaccess> in line with the rules of EAD in the descriptions of series of product catalogs held for one department store. An index of the products in these catalogs (e.g., gloves, hats, shoes) was prepared, with these index terms appearing as the <controlaccess> element. Users would, therefore, see different kinds of data in the same element of description. Although we recognized that this was not a particularly satisfactory compromise, it was the only element that could be adapted to encompass this relationship, so we chose to craft our local rules to use it for both purposes. It would have been possible for us to create a new element to link record-series descriptions to the descriptions of functions and activities; however, we wanted to ensure our descriptions were as compatible as possible with the accepted international standards.

The final relationship that a record series can have is with other record series. The "Related Units of Description" [ISAD(G): 3.5.3] and <related material> (EAD) element was suitable for linking between descriptions. We also used the "Administrative History" [ISAD(G): 3.2.2] and <bioghist> (EAD) element as necessary to provide an expanded narrative description of the relationship between two or more series of records. Although generally used at a fonds or subfonds level to describe the history of the records creator, we found this element of value at the series level to record information concerning the administration of the record series being described. This was particularly the case where a records series was used in conjunction with another. For example, the description of a series of funeral journals and general ledgers maintained by the staff of Wylie & Lochhead Ltd. uses the administrative history element to describe the way in which staff used the records—in this case, for the management of accounts that had not been paid.[8] It also includes details of the ways in which the funeral journal was used in conjunction with other records held in the archive, such as funeral order books and funeral insolvent ledgers.

However, describing the relationships between record series in these two ways (through two different elements) brought a duplication of information. In order to minimize this, we recorded a full account of the relationship within the "Administrative History" [ISAD(G): 3.5.3] and <bioghist> (EAD) element and a briefer explanation within the "Related Units of Description" [ISAD(G): 3.2.3] and <related material> (EAD) element.

ISAAR(CPF) and EAC do include elements allowing links to other descriptive components, so we were able to link company descriptions to the relevant record series through the "Relating Corporate Bodies, Persons and Families to Archival Materials and Other Resources" [ISAAR(CPF): chapter 6] and <resourcerel> (EAC) element. Similarly, the relationships between companies and people were easily made through the "Relationships" [ISAAR(CPF): 5.3] and <eacrel> (EAC) element. However, as discussed above, there is no element that allowed a link to descriptions of functions or activities. Rather, ISAAR(CPF) includes its own elements to describe these functions. At the start of the project, we made the decision to describe the relationships between companies and their functions through a link to the authority record for these functions. We used the "Relating Corporate Bodies, Persons and Families to Archival Materials and Other Resources" [ISAAR(CPF): chapter 6] and <funactrel> (EAC) element to describe and make these links.

However, as the cataloging of the archive progressed, we made a slight change to our practice. This change was prompted when we started describing individual administrative units within a company. The description of the Army & Navy Stores Ltd. (a company within the House of Fraser group) is linked to authority records for its Group Management Committee and its board of directors. In line with our plans for organization authority descriptions, details of these units' functions should only have been represented as links to the relevant function authority descriptions. However, at the level of the administrative unit within a company, the potential value of an overview of the functions of the unit was recognized. We felt that we could use the "Functions, Occupations and Activities" [ISAAR(CPF): 5.2.5] and <funactdesc> (EAC) element to provide information on the particular role of the unit in carrying out the relevant function(s) in a way that would be of benefit to users. So, descriptions of administrative units within a company have both links to the relevant function descriptions and an overview of the role of the unit in carrying out these functions.[9]

Finally, descriptions of the functions and activities were created in accordance with ISDF using the EAF prototype. ISDF and EAF provided suitable elements of description for linking functions and activities to the relevant descriptions. Links to companies were recorded through the "Relating Functions to Corporate Bodies, Archival Materials and Resources" (ISDF: chapter 6) and <eacrel> (EAF) element. Links to other functions and activities used the "Relationships" (ISDF: 5.3) and <funactrel> (EAF) element. Lastly, activities were linked to record series through the "Relating Functions to Corporate Bodies, Archival Materials and Resources" (ISDF: chapter 6) and <resourcerel> (EAF) element.

Thus, by thinking creatively, we were able to adapt existing content and encoding standards to meet the way we wanted to catalog the House of Fraser Archive. We used the XML editor oXygen for both the development of the DTDs and the encoding of each descriptive component (descriptions of series, people, organizations, functions, and activities). As the cataloging itself progressed, some changes were made to the rules set out at the start of the project, but the DTDs for the descriptions themselves proved robust.

Our first step in developing authority records for the relevant functions for the House of Fraser Archive was to identify the functions and activities of the retail sector as a whole. In DAC, the function and activity descriptions for Scottish Higher Education had been based on the JISC Higher Education Business Classification Scheme.[10] As no such generic model of the retail sector was available, we undertook work to develop our own.

The high-level classification set out in various business and industrial classification schemes allowed us to define the industry and identify the broad terms (such as governance, merchandising, purchasing and procurement, and supply chain management) that sat at the top of our model.[11] A literature review of business administration also helped to define broad terms but lacked the necessary detail that we felt was required to offer the added value to our users. On reassessing the JISC business classification, we found that many of the functions included are not unique to the higher education sector and applied equally well to the business world. This, alongside a review of the House of Fraser's website, literature, and the archive itself, helped us to add the detail required for a workable model for the cataloging project. To ensure wider application across the retail and business sectors, the draft model was reviewed by a business expert at the university before being finalized.[12]

In applying the retail-sector function model, we planned to develop a single set of descriptions for the functions and activities of the House of Fraser and apply these across the archive. Links would be made, as appropriate, to the relevant organizations, people, and record-series descriptions. We started by looking at the core parent company, the House of Fraser, to develop function descriptions. Our initial attempts were successful. The description of a function was applicable to each of the relevant House of Fraser organizations, dating from 1849 to the present day. However, when we looked to link this description to the other companies within the archive (those not a part of the core parent company), it was not a true representation of the way in which this function was performed. This is primarily due to the nature of the House of Fraser group. Although founded in 1849, the majority of the 200 individual department stores represented in the archive were acquired as active businesses in the 20th century. Although all the department stores carried out the same functions, they did not all perform them in the same way. We were, then, unable to use a description of a function based on the way in which the core House of Fraser parent company performed a function to accurately describe the performance of the same function by one of its subsidiaries. We realized that we would have to develop function descriptions for each individual department store.

This realization brought challenges for the project. Primarily, this was one of resources. Creating descriptions of the functions and activities of a business is time consuming. There was no scope within the project timeline to produce these descriptions for every individual company represented in the House of Fraser Archive. Our compromise was to concentrate on areas where description of functions and activities would be of most value to users. The archive includes, for example, a large number of accounting records that can be difficult for users (and archivists) to understand. We prioritized, therefore, by developing function and activity descriptions that explained financial management and financial accounting to assist users in understanding the records. These descriptions were developed for 10 organizations across the archive.

The final part of the project was to develop the online catalog. For the technical development, the University of Glasgow's Humanities Advanced Technology and Information Institute provided consultancy services to build a custom-designed system. In addition to the technical development of the site, the project team also considered issues surrounding the presentation of the descriptive components and the discovery options for users.

The online catalog was planned as a series of linked descriptions. Each authority or record-series description would be displayed as its own webpage, linking out to the related descriptions. We started to consider their presentation as our cataloging work produced descriptions with significant numbers of links. This was particularly evident as descriptions of the larger companies represented in the Houser of Fraser Archive were developed. These companies have lots of related record series, companies, and people. Having all of these links displayed creates very long webpages. This drove us to consider the presentation of the record-series information as a priority.

For example, our initial plan was that there would be no particular order to the listing of related record series. They would be added simply in the order they were cataloged. However, as cataloging progressed, we became concerned that the lack of any order would be unhelpful to users. Our first attempt at imposing an order was to list the records series chronologically. This worked well for companies with a small number of related record series, as the display could be quickly scanned. However, it proved less useful for those companies with larger numbers of related record series. We felt further organization in the display of the records was necessary to assist the user. We were, however, aware of the risk that we would be replacing the rigid, monohierarchical structure of a fonds-based description with another rigid structure. Our compromise was to establish a set of nine, very broad, function-based groups into which we arranged the record series for display within the company description. The groupings are: corporate records, legal records, financial records, operational records, merchandising records, marketing records, public relations records, staff records, and property records.

As noted, an aim of EtU was to develop a flexible catalog, one that would be capable of being explored in ways that suit each user's own preferences. We therefore had to ensure multiple discovery options within the online catalog. This meant having more than a simple free-text search. We saw the key to our flexible catalog in building on opportunities created by the archive's different descriptive components. We wanted to develop browsable lists both to provide an overview of the collection and offer multiple access points. To ensure that these lists were of most value to users, we based the topics on inquiries received by the service. Many of the lists suggested (company names, person names, places) could be generated from the five descriptive components. However, users also requested access to records by product, business type, and record type; automatically generating these lists relied on adding new index terms to descriptions.

These additional topics for browsable lists, based on patterns of user requests, were in contrast to our plans for the interface. Drawing on the findings of DAC, we had planned to avoid the use of subject indexes. DAC had discovered that users do not understand the principles that sit behind the development of subject indexes and are confused by them. However, we also recognized the need for the use of standard terms to guide users to records of potential interest. Therefore, we decided to add these three specific subject indexes for business, record, and product types. Each index is concerned with a narrow, well-defined subject area, and deals with a fairly concrete concept. This made us more confident that these specific indexes would offer less room for confusion over their scope and coverage than a single, general subject index.

Although limiting our own indexing to these narrow areas, we made the decision to embrace the opportunities offered by Web 2.0 technologies to allow users to develop indexes of their own design. On many social networks, user-defined indexes—created by user-created tags—work well. Therefore, our online catalog for the House of Fraser Archive offers users the option to log in and add tags to the descriptions to sit alongside the index terms we have provided. The catalog is also designed to allow users to add information to the descriptions by commenting. We hope that users will add further detail on the information held in particular records, highlight related resources, comment on the value or interpretation of particular record series, and add further detail about the companies and individuals described.

RESULTS

We believe EtU produced results that have significant potential to inform cataloging practice within the archives sector. For our archivist colleagues, the project developed a robust, scalable approach to cataloging, capable of describing the multiple contexts of an archive. All the relevant record series, companies, people, functions, and activities for the House of Fraser could be described using this methodology. Furthermore, the approach allows for the equal presentation of each context. One is not favored over another. Rather, the user is given information about all the contexts in which the record was created and used.

A significant advantage of the approach is its scalability. The descriptive components themselves are not fixed; additional elements of descriptions can be added in accordance with the relevant descriptive standards as required. There is no limit to the number of descriptions that can be included. Should accruals be received for the House of Fraser Archive, we will be able to add them to the catalog without the need for a restructuring or rearranging the descriptions. Similarly, should we wish to add further descriptions about the archive as it currently stands, for example, by adding additional descriptions of a company's functions, we will be able to do so.

We recognize, of course, that there are some issues with the cataloging methodology. For example, abandoning a fonds-level arrangement raises issues about recording information about the collection as a whole. Details such as the archival history of a collection, the immediate source of acquisition, and its appraisal are often best recorded at the fonds level as they apply across the collection. With no fonds-level description, the question arises as to where to record these important elements of archival description. One solution would be to include these details in each of the record-series descriptions. However, although in line with the principles of ISAD(G), this would lead to considerable levels of repetition across the catalog as a whole. Within the context of EtU, the catalog for the archive is delivered on its own website. This offers a potential solution, as it is possible to provide such information on the website, separate from the descriptions themselves. However, it remains unclear how this information could be recorded within a discovery system that provides access to the descriptions of many collections. We recognize that further research is required to identify other solutions to this problem. Investigation of a hybrid fonds–series system, where a fonds-level description would be added to the mix of descriptive components, is of particular interest.

The user perspective on the new approach to cataloging can be found in the results of the user testing carried out as part of EtU prior to the formal launch of the site, and in the use of the House of Fraser catalog since its official launch in December 2011. Unfortunately, due to delays in the development of the online catalog, only one round of user testing was completed. This was targeted at academics with a research interest in the archive. The test was a combination of initial questionnaire, controlled tests, free time to explore, and a semistructured interview. Five academics participated in the tests.

A significant issue relating to the presentation of search options was quickly identified among this group. Users did not understand the difference between the free-text search and the browsable lists. Their colocation on a single webpage led some users to try to combine the free-text search with a term from one of the lists. In addition, all users concentrated on the free-text search option, with the browsable lists little used.

Based on these results, the online catalog launched in 2011 has completely separate search and browse options.

In both the controlled tests and the free time to explore, all five users chose very different routes through the catalog. Users voiced their thoughts as they worked through these activities, allowing us to understand that each was using his or her own tried and tested search approaches. For us, this meant success: We had developed a flexible catalog that allowed people to use their own strategies easily. Presented with links to related descriptions of companies, people, and records, the majority of users followed these through. The users were able to access the information they required, working through the multiple contexts to discover the required descriptions. The testing highlighted that further guidance is required to enable users to fully exploit descriptions of functions and activities. Though they were noticed by some users, there was some uncertainty as to what they were.

While we made changes to the interface prior to launch as a result of this user testing, the current website has had no formal user testing. We can, however, look at users' interaction with the site to have some understanding of their experience. Around 200 people have registered on the site since its launch. Follow-up enquiries to Archive Services highlight that some users have the expectation that registering with the site will provide access to more content. We have disappointed users who are expecting digitized images of the archive. Other users have added comments to the site, the majority sharing memories of shopping at some of the stores or details of their ancestors who worked for the group. Others simply post their inquiries. Very few users, however, add tags to our catalog or add further detail to the descriptions of records after they have actually used them in our searchroom. We were aware when we included tagging and commenting functionality in the site that they will only have value after a critical mass of users contributes. Gaining such a number of users will require wider promotion of the site and further guidance on what we would like users to contribute.

LESSONS LEARNED

In our assessment, EtU was a successful project, generating positive results with the development of a new method for cataloging. However, our experience has taught us some valuable lessons that could benefit others who want to explore new approaches to cataloging.

In line with our standard cataloging practice, we used an XML editor to create the catalog data. Over the course of the project, templates for each type of description were developed, but each cataloger still had to ensure that the descriptive data was appropriately encoded to ensure its accurate display on the online catalog. As cataloging work got under way, we realized that this was not only time consuming but also had a high potential for error. This was particularly apparent when a large number of links to related descriptions were being encoded. Errors in the encoding for these links result in broken links on the online catalog. As we were successfully using an XML editor to create catalog data for our other collections, we had not anticipated these issues and so had not investigated any other cataloging systems in our project planning. Future projects implementing a cataloging methodology of separate, but linked, descriptive components should include the investigation of automated systems to generate and maintain descriptions and the links between them.

Further testing of the value of function and activity authority records is also required. User testing and staff experience from EtU has demonstrated that these descriptions can add significant value, at least in our business archives context. However, due to the issues discussed previously, our project ultimately tested only a small number of company-specific function and activity authority records. Our planning for the function and activity descriptions had not anticipated the level at which these descriptions needed to be created or the resources needed to create them. Future projects should consider if a comprehensive set of these functional descriptions is of more value to the user than the targeted descriptions we delivered.

As this project demonstrates, there is room for more investigation of the implementation of descriptive standards. EtU developed project rules for the implementation of these standards, which included local modifications of the standards as well as our modified XML DTDs. To ensure that the standards themselves develop in a way that allows flexible application across multiple methods of cataloging, more experimentation is required to assess what kinds of changes are needed. The results of this experimentation should feed into standards revision, allowing their development into robust, but flexible, tools for the profession.

Finally, embarking on this kind of project, designed to test innovative cataloging practices, requires careful consideration of the required resources. The right mix of an appropriate collection, professional expertise, and time is needed for development, testing, and implementation. Unfortunately, this consideration is not an exact science. From our experience, the time required to complete such a project cannot be underestimated. Our AHRC funding provided a three-year timeline in which we were able to develop and test the delivery of our cataloging system. However, we have had to continue some cataloging work and the development of an online interface beyond the project.

CONCLUSION

EtU was an exciting project for Archive Services. It proved that there is room for experimentation and development in something that is core to our professional life: archival description. Simply by widening the focus of our descriptive practice, we have developed an approach to cataloging that represents the contexts and contents of an archive equally.

The challenge is to build on the outcomes and recommendations of EtU and continue the development of the House of Fraser Archive model. Without the dedicated project team to undertake this work, the service continues to use the traditional, fonds-based model of arrangement and description. Unfortunately, securing the resources to undertake such development work is difficult. The AHRC Resource Enhancement Scheme that funded both descriptive practice projects at Archive Services has ended. As a service, and as a sector as a whole, we need to find ways of financing such important development work.

Clare Paterson *is senior archivist and college librarian at the University of Glasgow.*

NOTES

1. This study draws on Lesley Richmond and Victoria Peters's "Empowering the User: The Development of Flexible Archival Catalogues Final Report," Arts and Humanities Research Council, 2009, accessed August 21, 2013, http://housefraserarchive.ac.uk/about/.
2. Gateway to Archives of Scottish Higher Education, accessed June 12, 2013, www.gashe.ac.uk. Please note that development work is under way (summer 2013) to ensure links within the catalog are fully functional.
3. The online catalog is accessible at www.housefraserarchive.ac.uk, accessed June 12, 2013.
4. "Developing Archival Context Standards for Functions in the Higher Education Sector Final Report," Arts and Humanities Research Council, 2006, accessed August 15, 2013, www.gashe.ac.uk/news/final_report.pdf.
5. For examples of the record-series system, see New South Wales State Records Archives Investigator, accessed October 15, 2013, http://investigator.records.nsw.gov.au/; National Archives of Australia Commonwealth Record Series System, accessed October 15, 2013, http://recordsearch.naa.gov.au/SearchNRetrieve/Interface/SearchScreens/AdvSearchMain.aspx.
6. The map of entities is accessible at http://investigator.records.nsw.gov.au/Help.aspx?ID=1, accessed June 12, 2013.
7. For more information on these ICA standards, see www.ica.org/10206/standards/standards-list.html.
8. The catalog description for the funeral journals and general ledgers is accessible at www.housefraserarchive.ac.uk/series/?id=fras-252, accessed June 12, 2013.
9. The catalog description for the board of directors is available at www.housefraserarchive.ac.uk/company/?id=c2605; and for the Group Management Committee at www.housefraserarchive.ac.uk/company/?id=c2596, accessed June 12, 2013.

10. JISC Higher Education Business Classification Scheme, 3rd iteration, JISCinfoNet, accessed June 12, 2013, www.bcs.jiscinfonet.ac.uk/he/.

11. The project team consulted United Nations Statistics Division, *International Standard Industrial Classification of All Economic Activities* (1989); Office for National Statistics, *UK Standard Industrial Classification of Economic Activities* (2003); U.S. Office of Management and Budget, *North American Industry Classification System* (2002).

12. The Retail Function and Activity Model is appendix A of Richmond and Peters's "Empowering the User: The Development of Flexible Archival Catalogues Final Report," accessed August 21, 2013, http://housefraserarchive.ac.uk/about/.

TEN

Business as Usual

Integrating Born-Digital Materials into Regular Workflows

Jackie Dean and Meg Tuomala,
University of North Carolina at Chapel Hill

For the better part of the past two decades, when we received born-digital materials at the Wilson Special Collections Library at the University of North Carolina at Chapel Hill (UNC), usually in the form of floppy or compact discs, we numbered them, listed them in a finding aid, housed them in archival-quality boxes, and crossed our fingers that nobody would ever want to see them. But in the fall of 2011, several factors came together to give us the opportunity to process born-digital materials and make them available to researchers. This case study shows the evolution of our workflow for arranging and describing born-digital material and how we have tried to weave it into our existing practices to create a new model for processing hybrid collections and born-digital materials. Specifically, we use the papers of John Kenyon Chapman to illustrate how hybrid collections are processed, how we provide access to born-digital special collections materials, and how born-digital items are represented in our finding aids and digital repository.

We discuss our planning process—specifically, how existing digital collections and services workflows influenced our decisions; the implementation of this project, processing a hybrid collection of personal papers; the results of our effort and how Technical Services and Reference and Instructional Services staff had somewhat differing views on its success; and the lessons we learned from processing this collection and how it has influenced our born-digital work at Wilson Library.

PLANNING

First, we should provide some background information on two other digital programs at the UNC Libraries: the Digital Southern Historical Collection manuscripts digitization program and the Carolina Digital Repository (CDR). These existing projects heavily influenced how we framed, planned, and were able to carry out our own born-digital processing work.

The Digital Southern Historical Collection is "a large-scale digitization program that is designed to provide online access to entire manuscript collections or to substantial portions of collections."[1] Digitized content is delivered through the collection's finding aid by an inline link at the folder level that takes the researcher to the "folder" in CONTENTdm where the digitized content can be viewed.[2] By the fall of 2011, the Digital Southern Historical Collection had been in existence for almost two years and we knew that, for the most part, this method of delivering digital content worked for our users. We felt that we wanted to employ the same mode of delivery—links to digital content at the folder level—for *born-digital* collection materials. We thought that this would be the most efficient and logical way to provide access, as it mimics the way our analog materials are delivered to researchers in the reading room and preserves the collection's context.

The Carolina Digital Repository is "a digital archives for materials produced by members of the University of North Carolina at Chapel Hill community."[3] It not only is an institutional repository for scholarly work in the traditional sense, but it is also set up to support the preservation and access needs of born-digital materials from UNC's Wilson Special Collections Library. Knowing that born-digital objects would ultimately be delivered through the CDR, we felt that we needed to coordinate with repository staff to design a processing workflow that would meet both their needs and those of archival technical services staff.

Earnest conversations about born-digital materials in special collections began in a group known as the Wilson Digital Acquisitions Working Group (WDAWG). From 2009 to 2011, Wilson Library curators, the electronic records archivist, Technical Services staff, Research and Instructional Services staff (our Reference Department), and staff from Library and Information Technology, met regularly to discuss how born-digital materials would be handled by the special collections library and the relationship between special collections and the CDR. This group talked through potential workflows, drafted a framework for what documentation collecting archivists would need to guide them through digital donations, and developed special collections–specific functional specifications for the CDR. At this point, we didn't have any actual collections to use as a pilot and our discussions remained abstract, but it was a valuable exercise to puzzle through the various issues with a diverse group of librarians and archivists.

In the midst of these abstract discussions, things began to get more concrete. In the fall of 2010 and winter of 2011, UNC's electronic records archivist, Erin O'Meara, and Records Services archivist, Meg Tuomala, began ingesting born-digital and digitized materials into the CDR to pilot test the repository's ingest workflow. These pilot collections included special collections materials, such as digital photographs from UNC's History Department and preservation masters of Southern Folklife Collection recordings, as well as materials that were not from special collections, such as an archive of digital images from UNC's Research Labs of Archaeology. After ingesting these pilot collections into the CDR, Erin O'Meara recognized the need for a tool to prepare digital files for ingest into the CDR and create a repository-ready submission information package (SIP).[4]

Greg Jansen, one of the CDR developers, turned his attention to creating this tool: the Curator's Workbench.[5] The Workbench allows for the capture of digital files from the original media or location, the creation and labeling of digital folders, the arrangement of digital files into digital folders, and for the deletion of files and folders, all without altering the original digital files. Once the arrangement is set, the Workbench produces an ingest-ready SIP file that includes the digital files and associated metadata. Technical Services staff then alerts CDR staff that there is content ready to be ingested. Currently, CDR staff ingests the SIP into the CDR; however, very soon Technical Services staff will be able to initiate and complete the entire process, from capture, to arrangement and description, through ingest.

Wilson Library Technical Services staff became involved with the Curator's Workbench as it was being developed. Greg Jansen included Technical Services staff in early discussions about how its functionality would support archival practice. Shortly after the Workbench was developed, manuscripts processing coordinator Jackie Dean began using it to prepare born-digital oral history interviews for ingest into the CDR. The CDR serves as a "dark archive" for the archival masters of the audio recordings and the electronic transcript files. However, the digital oral history files did not need additional arrangement or description, so she was not using the full functionality of the Workbench with these materials.

Talking through the larger concepts of born-digital work in the WDAWG meetings and seeing the development of the Curator's Workbench set the stage for a small group in the Technical Services department to jump into born-digital arrangement and description. This group consisted of Erin O'Meara, Jackie Dean, and Patrick Cullom, Wilson Library's photographic archivist. We felt confident that we could apply what we knew about archival arrangement and description in the analog world to the digital realm using the Curator's Workbench. We also had the technical and moral support of Workbench developer Greg Jansen. This helped us get over our feelings of being too overwhelmed to start and see past our paralyzing fear of causing irreversible damage to unique materials.

We knew we had a safe place to put the stuff, we had a tool to use to prepare it, we knew how we wanted to deliver it to researchers, and we finally had the confidence to get started. We just needed something to process.

IMPLEMENTATION

We found our test case with the papers of John Kenyon Chapman, a local social justice activist, community organizer, and historian who passed away in 2009.[6] The Southern Historical Collection (SHC), a collecting unit of the Wilson Special Collections Library, acquired these papers shortly after his death.

Kenyon's papers arrived at the SHC in primarily analog formats, but included 27 compact discs of born-digital correspondence, writings, photographs, and audio and video recordings. One of the SHC's main collecting initiatives focuses on acquiring materials documenting social justice activism in the South. Thus, the Chapman collection was flagged for priority processing by the director of SHC, Tim West. Since the subject matter of the collection is central to the SHC's collecting mission, it became a perfect candidate for us to use to investigate and explore how to arrange and describe the born-digital materials along with the analog.

While the collection's subject matter initially motivated us to prioritize its processing, other key features made it a good test case. As mentioned above, the born-digital materials came to us on compact discs. We felt comfortable putting the discs into our desktop computers and working with the files. The collection came to us from Joyce Chapman, the creator's daughter, who is trained as an archivist. She made a backup copy of each disc for us in case of media failure or corruption, which allowed us to feel extra safe working with them. Joyce Chapman also selected the files for donation in close consultation with Biff Hollingsworth, the SHC's outreach and collecting archivist. Because of this, we knew we could accept into the collection all of the files on the discs, bypassing an in-depth initial appraisal. At this point, we did not have a workflow set up for safely examining born-digital files for appraisal; having this work done before the materials came to the SHC allowed us to jump ahead to processing. Finally, since Biff and Joyce worked so closely together, we were also provided with information about the content and provenance of the born-digital files that we might not have otherwise had the opportunity to get. This allowed us to focus on the mechanics of how we would do the arrangement and description and not spend time analyzing the content.

Technical Services staff began working on the born-digital materials after arranging and creating a finding aid for the analog papers, photographs, audio, and video. We still saw the born-digital materials as separate and thought we would be in a better position to handle them after working through the analog materials. By the time we began to investigate the born-digital files, we already had the analog portion collection organized into 11 series. We reviewed Joyce Chapman's inventory of the born-digital materials to see if the digital objects would fit in with the existing analog series or form their own all-digital series. We found that we would need to do both.

We decided to start with a discrete group of born-digital files that were unique in nature from anything in the analog materials: audio files. Joyce Chapman's description said that John Kenyon Chapman recorded them on a personal voice recorder in the year leading up to his death. Joyce's description also noted the topics of the recordings and the names of other people featured in the recordings. The audio files were arranged by Joyce into three folders, "Personal," "Political," and "Downloaded after Yonni Chapman's Death." (Yonni was Chapman's nickname.) We kept this arrangement and did not change the original audio file titles. Many of the audio file titles were descriptive—for example, "Notes for Town Hall meeting 23 March 09." For the audio file titles that were not descriptive, we felt comfortable keeping the original titles and asking researchers to rely on the provided series-level description or to listen to the audio file. We did not listen to the recordings.

We used the Workbench to view the arrangement of the audio files and make the determination that we would not rearrange or change the titles of the existing folders or audio files. The Workbench also allows for the inclusion of descriptive metadata at any level—file, folder, series, or collection. This description is captured as a MODS record and displays with the digital object in the CDR. We created the series title "Voice Recorder Audio Files" and a scope and content note at the series level based on Joyce's description of the files. We entered the series-level title and a scope and content note for the series into the Workbench's metadata editor. We exported a SIP for these materials and CDR staff ingested it into the CDR.

Now that we had experience preparing born-digital materials for ingest into the CDR under our belts, we turned our attention to how to best represent these materials in the collection's finding aid. We created a series in the EAD finding aid for "Voice Recorder Audio Files" following our usual template for descriptive elements at the series level. This template includes title, date, scope and content note, extent of items, and arrangement elements. For analog materials, we estimate the number of items based on the type and number of containers we use; the CDR provided the exact number of born-digital files. In the finding aid, we recorded the same series title and scope and content note that we had entered into the Workbench metadata editor. We based the date, 2009, on Joyce Chapman's description of the files. In the arrangement element, we noted that the original order had been maintained. Finally, we added a processing note to explain that these materials were received at the SHC on compact discs and that the donor's original file titles were retained.

Next, we listed the digital folders "Political," "Personal," and "Downloaded after Yonni Chapman's Death," as nested components under the series. Here we followed our usual encoding template for folders but used the container type "digfolder" in the <container> element instead of our usual "folder." As already noted, we wanted to follow the same access and delivery model as the Digital Southern Historical Collection, where the folder title is an inline link to digitized content in CONTENTdm. The difference is that, in our case, the folder link leads to the born-digital content in the CDR. We encoded the link to the digital folder in the CDR as an "extref" in the <container> element. An example of the EAD encoding of one of the digital folders is as follows:

```
<c02><did><container type="digfolder"><extref href=https://cdr.lib.unc.
edu/search?facets=path%3a4%2cuuid%3a75c36700-f619-404b-9e25-
3b6d969e5a5d%2c5>DF-5441/1</extref></container><unittitle>
Personal</unittitle></did></c02>
```

When we transformed the finding aid into HTML using our XSLT stylesheet, we were pleased to see that the folders were linked and clicking on them took us into the contents of the digital folder in the CDR.

Testing the workflow with this small group of files highlighted a need to revise how we present description of the born-digital materials in the CDR. Originally, we intended to duplicate the descriptive elements from the finding aid to include in the CDR display. To that end, we included the scope and content note describing the Voice Recorder Audio Files series in both the CDR display and in the finding aid. We soon realized that because we update description fairly frequently because of changes or additions, we did not want to have to manually update descriptive metadata in the finding aid and the CDR. In the future, CDR staff plans to automate the updating of descriptive metadata in the CDR when the finding aid is updated, but for now we decided not to include any additional descriptive elements in the CDR display; the CDR contains simply a list of the born-digital folders. Essentially, the CDR display is analogous to opening up all of the containers and seeing all the folders in a collection: A researcher sees folder titles and is likely able to tell from these folder titles what collection he or she is looking at, and perhaps, the series. But in order to more thoroughly navigate a collection, the researcher will still need to use the finding aid. We proceeded through the rest of the born-digital material processing in the Chapman collection with the philosophy that all description would occur in the finding aid, and we did not use the MODS editor in the Workbench beyond recording folder titles.

The next group of born-digital materials that we worked with was Chapman's digital photographs, totaling around 350 images. With a few exceptions, the photographs were not arranged into folders and did not come with extra description from Joyce Chapman. Wilson Library's photographic archivist Patrick Cullom reviewed the images using a file browser on his computer because at this point, the Workbench only allowed us to view one image at a time, and using it as a file viewer would have been exceedingly time consuming. Patrick determined that most of the digital photographs in the collection were of a different nature than the analog photographs. The analog photographs primarily document demonstrations, speeches, meetings, and events with which Chapman was involved. The digital photographs are of a more personal nature and show Chapman with friends and family as well as scanned images of childhood photographs and digital photographs of nature scenes taken by Chapman. Around 50 of the digital photographs document protests and did fit topically with the analog photograph series.

After reviewing the images outside of the Workbench, Patrick determined broad categories in which to sort them. We then used the Workbench's arrangement section to create digital folders and labeled them with the names of the categories that Patrick determined: "Photographs of Yonni Chapman, circa 1947–1980s" (these were primarily scanned images), "Photographs of Yonni Chapman, circa 1990s–2009," "Photographs of Yonni Chapman with Family and Friends," and "Photographs by Yonni Chapman." Using the arrangement feature in the Workbench, we sorted the images into these folders. Beyond the folder titles, we did not record any description of the digital photographs in the Workbench; therefore, none are displayed in the CDR.

As with the Voice Recorder Audio Files series, we followed our regular practice for recording series-level elements. We titled the series "Personal Photographs" and included an extremely brief scope and content note. We felt that in the short term, researchers would be less interested in Chapman's personal life than in his documentation of social justice activism. At the series level, we include a processing note saying that the digital photographs arrived at the SHC unsorted and were grouped into these categories during processing. We nested the digital folder titles within the series. We opted not to add any additional information about the images at the folder level. We followed the same practice of including a link to the digital folder in the CDR.

The approximately 50 digital images of demonstrations and protests gave us the opportunity to integrate digital folders into the list of analog folders in the finding aid. The analog photographs arrived at the SHC grouped into folders by Chapman centering on protests, events, or demonstrations. The folders were then arranged chronologically within the series by processing staff. As previously noted, Chapman did not group the digital photographs into folders. After determining that this group of born-digital images was not personal in nature like the majority of the digital photographs described in the Personal Photographs series and were more similar in content to the analog photographs, Patrick carefully examined the images and grouped them by event. He did some research to determine an appropriate folder title and the date for each event-based grouping. Following what was now becoming our regular practice, Patrick created folders in the Workbench, recorded the titles that he had determined, and created a SIP that was then ingested into the CDR. We listed the digital folders in the finding aid where they fit chronologically in the existing analog photograph series. The digital folder's description looks almost identical to an analog folder in the finding aid, except that the digital folder links to the digital materials in the CDR.

Finally, there were two compact discs containing scans of photographs and other materials relating to past civil rights events. We treated each compact disc as a digital folder, created a title for the digital folder after reviewing the contents, and ingested these materials into the CDR. These digital folders are listed in the finding aid at the end of the analog photograph series. A processing note is included at the folder level saying that the materials came to the SHC on a compact disc. We also include a transcription of the text from the disc's label in the scope and content note.

The third major category of born-digital materials in the John Kenyon Chapman papers contained files of primarily Microsoft Word documents collected by Joyce from Chapman's laptop and the contents of an external hard drive that had been burned onto compact discs. These came with brief descriptions from Joyce—primarily a directory listing for the laptop files. The files from the external hard drive dated from 2004 to 2005, and the files from the laptop dated from 2008 to 2009. For the most part, the files were grouped into folders and labeled by Chapman. The content ranges from drafts of letters relating to political organizing to personal journals regarding his illness.

Many files from the external hard drive and laptop, especially those relating to social justice organizing, could be grouped intellectually with materials in the analog series. Though we felt comfortable doing this type of integration after our experience integrating the digital photographs into the analog series, we decided that it would be too time consuming to analyze each digital file and determine where it might fit in the existing analog series arrangement. Instead, we decided to have an all-digital series for the external hard drive files and one for the laptop files. Rather than creating series titles reflecting the content of the files, we decided to go with "External Hard Drive Files" and "Laptop Files" as series titles. Again we followed our usual template for series-level descriptive elements and crafted a very brief scope and content note for each series based largely on Chapman's folder titles.

As we progressed, we acknowledged and accepted that there would be inconsistencies between folder titles in the finding aid and in the CDR. In the Voice Recorder Audio Files series, we tested using the folder titles supplied by Joyce Chapman in the finding aid, albeit on a very small scale. In that series, we kept the folder titles and listed them in the finding aid without changing them at all; there were only three folders and their titles were very simple—"Personal," "Political," and "Downloaded after Yonni Chapman's death." In contrast, Chapman's original digital folder titles in the "External Hard Drive Files" and "Laptop Files" series were somewhat cryptic in many cases—for example, "Nov.13 T&R demo." We decided to follow the same practice we use in recording analog folder titles in finding aids. We do not transcribe the creator's exact titles; we take what is there and apply our institutional style guide, which often means changing dates to a day-month-year format and spelling out abbreviations for the sake of searchability and access. Following Erin O'Meara's advice, we decided not to change the original folder titles on the digital folders in the CDR, revising them only in the description found in the finding aid. Therefore, the folder title in the finding aid reads "Greensboro Truth and Reconciliation Commission demonstration, 13 November 2004"; however, when the link is followed to the CDR, Chapman's original title "Nov.13 T&R demo" is used.

We realize that this is somewhat challenging for the researcher, and we hope that a future enhancement to the CDR will allow for the automatic inclusion of the archivist-generated title as it appears in the finding aid as well as the creator's original title, when they differ.

In addition to challenging the researcher, we recognize that leaving the unedited original folder titles and opting not to add any additional descriptive elements beyond the folder titles in the CDR seriously limits the functionality of the CDR as an access and discovery tool for born-digital special collections materials. Currently, we are operating as though users will not discover born-digital materials without first going through the finding aid, but we also realize that this is a naïve and oversimplified view of how our researchers find our materials. There is no clear explanation in the CDR that the Chapman materials are part of a larger, hybrid body of materials, and there is no link now to get from the CDR to the finding aid. We acknowledge that the assumption that all users will begin with the finding aid will have to change. As more content becomes available in the CDR, we will not be able to take for granted that users will start with the finding aid; we will need to consider that users will begin to discover material through the CDR.

By November of 2012, we completed the processing of Chapman's born-digital materials, and uploaded the John Kenyon Chapman Papers finding aid to the Wilson Library's website.

RESULTS

Wilson Library Technical Services staff considers the project to be a success because we moved from talking and theorizing about born-digital arrangement and description to actually doing it; the difficulty in making that leap should not be underestimated. Having a collection with born-digital materials that was deemed high priority for processing motivated us to learn the mechanics of arrangement in Curator's Workbench and to determine how best to represent the content in our finding aids. Since the appraisal and some identification of the born-digital files were done for us by the donor, the Chapman files could be considered a less complex processing endeavor. We do feel, however, that the basic workflow that we used for this collection can be adapted and expanded for other born-digital materials in the future. Perhaps most importantly, we confirmed that the fundamental thought processes that we bring to analog material could be transferred to the born-digital realm, giving us the confidence to keep tackling these collections

The reaction from our Reference and Instruction staff to this initial offering was mixed. Reference and Instruction staff is very much in favor of the born-digital content being delivered via a link at the folder level in the same way as the digitized archival material in the Digital Southern Historical Collection; however, since the back-end systems used for the born-digital and digitized are different, the finding aids with digitized content behave slightly differently. Namely, the finding aids with digitized materials (accessed through CONTENTdm) include a notification at the top of the finding aid that clearly signifies that some of the collection materials have been digitized. Also, a list of finding aids with digitized content is generated automatically and is included on the Digital Southern Historical Collection homepage. Currently, neither of these behaviors occurs for the finding aids for collections that contain born-digital content (accessed through the CDR). When Technical Services staff began processing the born-digital materials in the Chapman papers, we didn't take into consideration that this would be problematic. After talking with Reference and Instruction staff, we agree that born-digital and digitized materials should present themselves in all of our descriptive systems in the same manner and we will work toward this in the future.

LESSONS LEARNED

One of the most significant lessons learned by those of us in Technical Services is to be more confident about and keep processing born-digital materials and hybrid collections. We found that the more we did the work of born-digital arrangement and description, the more we learned how to do it. And the more we learned how to do it, the more we are able to think of ways to do it better, streamline our workflows, and make suggestions to CDR staff for improvements that could be made to the Curator's Workbench and the CDR.

As noted above, since the Chapman materials came to the SHC with the close mediation of Biff Hollingsworth, the collecting and outreach archivist, we skipped our typical first step of having collection staff appraise the materials. However, as a result of using Curator's Workbench for arrangement, we were able to conceptualize how the collecting staff could use the Workbench to do appraisal when materials are initially accessioned. We realized that in order for materials to be appraised by collecting staff and for this work to be captured and transferred to Technical Services staff, the Workbench would need to support projects being started by collectors on their computers, closed and set aside, and then opened back up by Technical Services staff on different computers. This functionality has now been built into Curator's Workbench, but at this point we haven't tested it. We would also like to explore capturing appraisal and accessioning notes within the Workbench rather than having this information in a separate document or in an accession record.

With the Chapman papers, we ingested the materials into the CDR and then were able to derive the URLs to include in our EAD encoding that would link the folder in the finding aid description to the digital folder in the CDR. We cut and pasted the links by hand into our EAD finding aid which we author in oXygen. At our request, Greg Jansen added functionality to the Workbench that allows the export of the folder titles and URLs as a comma-separated value file that we can easily incorporate into our EAD markup. This has significantly streamlined the mechanics of getting the links from the CDR into our finding aids.

Finally, we had to relearn the lesson that archival description should not be done in a processing vacuum, whether the materials are analog or digital. Now that we have the mechanics of these processes worked out, we need to talk with Reference and Instruction staff about how to present the digital objects. We will work toward having the finding aids with born digital content behave in the same manner as finding aids with digitized content. Perhaps more importantly, we will need to work together to solve the larger interface problems of navigating between the finding aid and the content in the CDR. Once again, the access model for digitized materials might offer a solution. Our Library and Information Technology developers are working to incorporate inline digitized images into the finding aid, so users do not have to leave it to see the digitized content. We hope that the same techniques can be used for our born-digital content.

CONCLUSION

Our guiding philosophy at the Wilson Special Collections Library at UNC has been to treat born-digital materials as much as possible in the same way as we treat analog materials. In other words, we will maintain our practice of focusing on aggregate description, weighing the impact that more or less arrangement will have on access and discovery, and letting the finding aid knit together all of the parts of an archival collection, whether they are analog, digitized, or born-digital. At UNC, the tools and systems we use to do this work allow us to put our philosophy into practice. As already described, currently once materials are ingested into the CDR, their metadata and arrangement cannot be changed without the involvement of a CDR administrator. CDR staff will soon be adding the capability for Technical Services staff to arrange and describe born-digital materials once they have been ingested into the CDR. This is a particularly exciting development for those of us in archival processing because it allows us to employ an iterative style of processing for both our born-digital and our analog materials. Typically, with our analog collections, we attempt to make the materials usable without committing extensive processing resources. If it becomes clear that we have not performed an effective processing treatment on a collection or any of its parts, we revise our original arrangement or description. It is a relief that with our born-digital materials we will soon have the freedom to revisit our decisions and go back and make adjustments over a collection's evolution and use, just as we do with our analog collections.

While we have emphasized the commonalities between our analog processing procedures and mind-sets and born-digital processing, we also need to focus on what is different. As mentioned above, we used our existing descriptive template at the series and folder levels to describe born-digital folders in the finding aid. We made some concessions to their digital nature, noting that the materials came to us on compact disc, but it is unclear at this point if that information is useful or necessary. As more description of born-digital materials becomes available, we will need to determine what should be communicated about these formats to users. And, of course, our processing guidelines will need to evolve to reflect this.

All in all, what has been most significant for us has been the ability to jump in and try this work. The Curator's Workbench developers and the CDR staff's encouragement of our experimentation (and their help when we hit roadblocks) were essential for completing the processing of the

John Kenyon Chapman papers. This supportive environment has allowed us to make progress in our workflows and build our confidence in handling these materials. As all of us in the profession know, at this point, there is no turning back. At UNC, we've learned that the way forward is through trial and error, conversation, and relying on the fundamentals of good arrangement and description.

Jackie Dean *is the manuscripts processing coordinator and* ***Meg Tuomala*** *is the electronic records archivist at The Wilson Special Collections Library at the University of North Carolina at Chapel Hill.*

NOTES

1. "About," Digital Southern Historical Collection, UNC University Libraries, accessed October 25, 2013, http://dc.lib.unc.edu/cdm/archivalhome/collection/ead.
2. See an example of inline linking to digitized archival material in the finding aid for the Cameron Family Papers, www2.lib.unc.edu/mss/inv/c/Cameron_Family.HTML.
3. "About the Repository," Carolina Digital Repository, accessed October 25, 2013, https://cdr.lib.unc.edu/scontent/aboutPages/aboutTheRepository.xml.
4. For an overview of CDR Ingest workflow see "Technology Overview," Carolina Digital Repository, accessed October 25, 2013, https://cdr.lib.unc.edu/scontent/aboutPages/techOverview.xml.
5. Martin Gengenbach, "About the Curator's Workbench," Carolina Digital Repository blog, July 14, 2011, http://blogs.lib.unc.edu/cdr/index.php/about-the-curators-workbench.
6. "Finding Aid for the John Kenyon Chapman Papers," Southern Historical Collection, accessed October 25, 2013, www2.lib.unc.edu/mss/inv/c/Chapman,John_Kenyon.html.

ELEVEN

Opening the Black File Cabinets

Describing Single Items for Discovery and Access

James Gerencser, Dickinson College

Like many repositories today, the Archives and Special Collections at Dickinson College present us with challenges resulting from earlier acquisitions and cataloging practices. In our case, during the mid-20th century, the librarian responsible for the special collections received catalogs and personal notices from manuscript dealers regarding letters, ephemera, and other materials that might be of interest. From these catalogs, the librarian routinely purchased individual documents—primarily, 18th- and 19th-century letters of noted alumni, faculty members, trustees, and local figures. The librarian also acquired items related to British and American politicians and literary figures, in the expectation that they might be useful to professors and students.

At the same time, alumni and descendants of alumni contributed items of their own, making gifts of single documents they found interesting that had belonged to an ancestor. Personal letters between students and family members, grade reports, tuition vouchers, and programs for campus events were donated and added to the collections. Through the years, these many one-item donations and purchases came to comprise a somewhat large group of "stuff"—roughly three thousand items—housed in individual file folders within a series of black file cabinets in the special collections vault.

In the 1950s, the practice for describing these materials was to create one or more catalog cards for them, which were then filed in the handsome card catalog in the reading room. A main entry or author card, along with a few additional subject or "see" reference cards, provided a simple means of discovery. Over time, a handful of typed subject guides, which included these single items as well as select materials from our traditional collections of personal papers, were developed on a few particularly popular topics as a more convenient way to help researchers get beyond the card catalog.

Once professionally trained archivists were hired during the latter quarter of the century, finding aids were created to describe our collections of personal papers. With the development of an online public access catalog (OPAC) for the library, MARC records were created based on these finding aids. The library's online catalog, as well as OCLC WorldCat, now offered computer-based means to discover collections. However, while finding aids and new online catalogs provided ways to encourage discovery of collections of materials, the individually cataloged items in the black file cabinets were not added to the OPAC and so remained discoverable only through the card catalog or the increasingly out-of-date subject guides.

With the development of our first website around the turn of the 21st century, our top priority was, quite naturally, to post our finding aids online, sharing descriptions and inventories of whole collections. In a short time, most of the materials in these collections were discoverable to people around the world via simple keywords entered into a search engine. After only a few years, the number of requests being received from off-site researchers increased fivefold as a result of our finding aids being available online.

In contrast, the items in the black file cabinets could still only be found by patrons visiting the reading room and using the obsolete card catalog despite the fact that we had had an online presence for more than 10 years. Items that aren't easy to find certainly aren't likely to be used, so the question we asked ourselves was how could we make these single items more discoverable in a web-based environment? And perhaps just as important, how could we do so in a relatively efficient and effective manner but still within the constraints of our limited available resources?

PLANNING

Our solution to "opening" the contents of the black files cabinets has its roots—although somewhat circuitously—in our previous efforts to explore using new technologies to increase the discoverability of our collections. In April 2007, with the assistance of colleagues in the Academic Technology Services Department, the staff of the Archives and Special Collections Department launched a new kind of blog. This blog, utilizing Drupal software, provides an online space in which we can briefly describe recent research requests from off-site patrons. The staff-only side of the blog is used to record contact information for researchers, the search trail followed in efforts to respond to the research need, and the location of relevant resources that are ultimately identified. The public-facing side of the blog features a brief description of the topic of the research query along with relevant subject tags and is fully discoverable by search engines. The blog entries thus serve as new access points by which researchers might be able to discover our resources.[1]

Within a year of its launch, this reference blog had proven itself a success. Items that had previously been hard to find, seemingly buried within a lengthy finding aid or perhaps not specifically mentioned at all within a less detailed inventory, could now be found due to the effectiveness of search engines. If a reference blog post mentioned a relevant author or the title of some particular piece of content, future researchers could be led to the same resources. A prime example of the value of the reference blog is an item from one of our many collections regarding Three Mile Island. Researchers on this topic are often interested in Hyman Rickover's commissioned report on the Three Mile Island accident, which is not widely available. We received our first reference request for a copy of the report in early 2008 and duly logged that request on the reference blog. Because that reference request is now more easily discoverable by search engines, we have received repeated requests for that report from other researchers. Thanks to the reference blog, items that previously may have been little used because they were hard to find are now being discovered and used by multiple researchers.

Besides the utility of the reference blog for aiding discovery, the retrieval of frequently requested materials has been made more efficient. With each subsequent request on the same topic, staff members can simply check the private side of the blog post for the location of the relevant resources, pull these items from their shelf locations, and then copy or scan them for the latest researcher. The very nature of these repetitive requests, however, made us want to find a better way to share copies of these now more popular materials. It would save staff time if each subsequent researcher could simply download a digital copy of the item rather than need to ask staff for assistance. Couldn't we scan the item upon the occasion of the first request and then upload the file to an online location where it could be briefly described, discovered via future searches, and accessed directly by others interested in the same topic? We would then have a virtual repository of individual items that had been requested by our users—a demand-driven online collection.

With that idea firmly in mind, we then considered the plight of the 3,000 single-item gifts and purchases of the black file cabinets.[2] Besides providing access to documents that had been requested by researchers and digitized on demand, we could also digitize and describe these documents that were essentially hidden to an online world. This would solve the problem of how to make these materials more easily discoverable.

Given our favorable experience with the reference blog serving as a discovery tool, we decided this was something worth trying.

This, then, was our goal—we wanted to build an online tool that was essentially a "catablog" for individual items.[3] This document blog would provide easy access to digitized items and would at the same time provide basic descriptive information about those items. The individual blog posts, once crawled, would be easily discoverable through search engines, but would also be searchable directly through the archives website. The documents that were digitized to satisfy a research request could be linked from the reference blog post and could also be linked to any relevant finding aids or other resources. Finally, the simplicity of the blog format would make the site easily understandable and accessible to most users.

Using the simple blog format to describe these items had another important advantage. The Archives and Special Collections Department is staffed by two full-time professionals and one full-time paraprofessional. The volume of research requests received from on campus and off, the amount of instruction done in support of the curriculum, and the various administrative responsibilities required mean that there is little time available for these three permanent employees to arrange and describe collections. As a result, undergraduate work/study students and interns perform almost all of the processing activities, with permanent staff in supervisory roles. Thus, one important consideration in designing the new document blog was to ensure that the work of digitization, description, and upload could be effectively performed by our undergraduate workforce.

In considering what tool to use to support our needs for this project, we made our choice relatively quickly. The open-source content management software Drupal had already been used by undergraduate work/study students and interns with great success on more than one project within the archives, including our "Women's Experiences at Dickinson College" blog.[4] Drupal was also being used for our reference blog, and so we were familiar with both the capabilities and the flexibility of this tool through our experiences with these and other projects over the previous few years. Colleagues in Academic Technology had a great deal of expertise with the software as well, and we knew we could rely on their assistance for training and support when needed. Finally, the sizeable active user community for Drupal provided assurances that the software would continue to thrive and enjoy strong support for the foreseeable future. For these reasons, we did not feel the need to spend much time exploring various other software options for our new document blog.

Having made the decision to utilize Drupal for the document blog, we needed to consider how we would configure our metadata. Among the desirable aspects of Drupal is the ability to design each individual blog from scratch, choosing what metadata fields to create, what format the information in those fields should take, and how that information should be entered and displayed. After deciding upon a metadata configuration, we would just need to convey that information to our Academic Technology colleagues so that they could do the necessary programming to set up this new blog for us.

We started with the idea that, as a baseline, we would want to replicate the information available in the old card catalog. Each of the old catalog cards included an author or title as a main entry, some form of date, a brief description, notes about donation or acquisition, and a call number. If nothing else, we should at least provide the same level of discoverability that was available to patrons in our reading room.

The title of the blog post itself seemed the best analogy to the main entry, so we decided that would serve as our anchor. If the item was a letter, we decided that the title of the post should include the author as well as the intended recipient of the letter. For a speech or essay, we decided to include the author and a portion of the title, or else the author and the main topic of the essay in cases where the title might not suggest the content of the essay.

We decided that the open text field should provide the only opportunity for a narrative description of the item. The card catalog information would provide a baseline for initial entry, but the person entering the metadata could expand upon that information as necessary. The descriptive entry could be as little as a phrase or sentence, or as much as a few paragraphs describing the document. Like all the fields, the description could be easily edited, either to make corrections to the existing entry or to add further information when it became available.

The call number was provided to facilitate retrieval of the original item upon request. The donation and other acquisition information offered the patron a clue about the provenance of the item—how and when it entered the special collections—while also recognizing the donor for his or her contributions to the special collections.

For the date field, we decided to display the date in a fuller form by spelling out each month. In doing so, we wanted to avoid any ambiguity and confusion that could result if dates were presented using only numbers or abbreviations. We also chose to create a second date field, one that would not display to the user. This field expressed the date in a computer-readable format. The sorting and displaying of information in chronological order, when desired, would be made possible using this second date field.

Once we had settled upon the fields that replicated the card catalog information, we began considering tag fields that might allow for some of the types of browsing and sorting that patrons typically request, such as: What items can be found in the collections regarding military actions during the Revolutionary War? What letters or diaries do you have that talk about student life at the college? What materials do you have from the late 19th century reflecting gender roles and relationships within families? Based on the types of reference questions we have received over the years, being able to represent general time periods, different types of materials, and broad subject areas all seemed like they may be useful for our patrons.

We first created a "People" tag as a way to build a natural index over time. For a letter, the author, recipient, and any individuals discussed in the letter could easily be tagged. For lengthier sources, like a diary or autograph book, tags for people might have to be reserved for individuals more frequently mentioned or more prominently presented. The most important aspect of the People tag would be the ability for researchers to find additional materials by or about a specific person with ease once they had found a blog post relevant to their initial query.

We next developed a "Subject" tag field. Although we discussed the possibility of this field supporting free-text entry, we ultimately decided that the wide variety of terms likely to be used by different student workers to describe the same object would lead to few tags being used multiple times, thus defeating their purpose. In the end, we developed a list of roughly 20 broad subject areas (e.g. Business and Industry, Health and Medicine, Travel and Tourism) combined with a few narrower subject areas particularly well represented in our collections (e.g., Carlisle and Cumberland County, Dickinson College Student Affairs, Three Mile Island). By limiting subjects to these specific predetermined options, there could be greater assurance of students applying the terms in a consistent manner. In addition, if further subject options seem warranted by the addition of new materials, this list can easily be expanded.

To allow some general filtering by date, we created a "Time Period" tag field. Broken into 20-year increments, this field allows researchers to easily identify materials within the same basic time frame. When combined with other tag fields or with a keyword search, the Time Period can offer a useful way to sort or limit results as desired. Finally, in order to allow researchers the ability to narrow searches to particular information types (e.g., Diaries and Journals, Broadsides and Posters, Music), we created the "Format" tag field (see figure 11.1).

The last element to add to our metadata configuration was an image of the item itself. We opted to include a basic image of the item presented in JPG format. This image would not only provide some visual interest to the blog posts, but would also aid the researcher in deciding if this particular item was of use or interest. In addition, we included the option of uploading a complete digital surrogate of the original document as a PDF file in order to provide immediate access to materials.

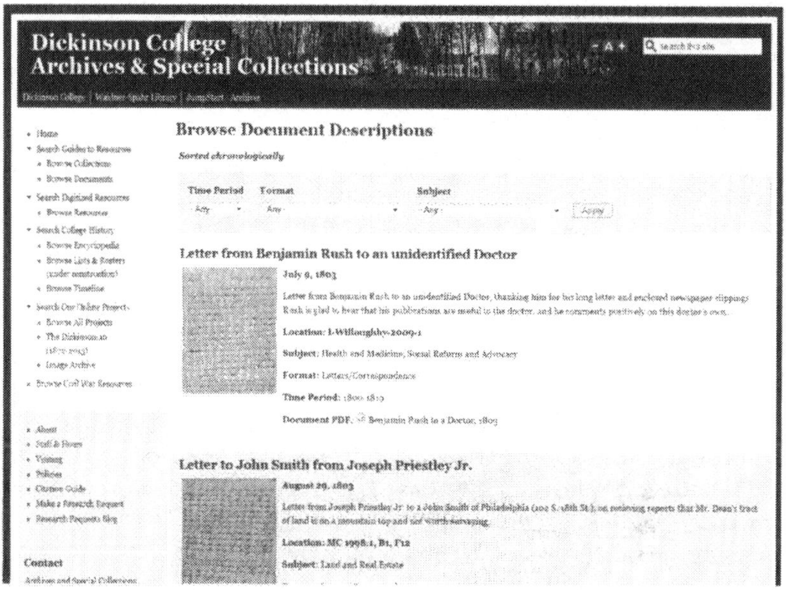

Figure 11.1. Browse screen for the document blog, showing options to sort entries by time period, format, or subject.

IMPLEMENTATION

As should be clear, this project was one that was undertaken in a somewhat informal manner. An advantage of working in a small organization is that we are encouraged to develop creative, low-cost solutions to local challenges, and we are relatively free to explore new tools as we see fit. Since minimal resources were required, we were able to proceed without developing a formal project schedule. As this was an experiment, we did not map out a long-term strategy for exporting or reusing the descriptive data from the blog posts, nor did we plan for the Drupal blog to interface with any other systems, except by means of simple hyperlinks. Our only intention and goal for the document blog was that it successfully increase the discoverability of these individual items by leveraging the power of search engines to connect users with our resources.

Once we had decided upon our initial metadata configuration for the blog, all we needed to do was set up a meeting with our colleagues in the Academic Technology Services Department who manage the server environment on which our Drupal instance operates. We discussed our idea and explained the specifications for the different text and tag fields. Within a week of that meeting, the basic framework for our document blog had been created. After reviewing this first iteration, we ironed out some details regarding how the different text and tag fields should be ordered on the web form that our undergraduate workers would fill out. We also made some adjustments to the basic site design and decided how the various metadata fields would display to the user. After these changes, we were ready to begin entering information in order to test our metadata schema and display.

Because of our past experience with Drupal, archives staff members felt confident in being able to make minor changes to tag fields. For example, as we began to enter test data, we recognized the need for a few additional subject options and simply added them to our list of selections. We made additional minor changes such as these during our initial testing. Again, one of the reasons we decided to use Drupal for this blog was the flexibility of the software and the ease with which we could implement changes.

Once we felt we had entered enough sample data, we considered how this information was being presented to the user. How could we ensure that the most crucial information was foregrounded and noticeable? What sizes and styles of font would be most effective? What labels should be applied to data fields to make them intelligible to most patrons? As we considered questions such as these, we approached our own student workers for feedback. While perhaps not as effective as forming focus groups of people unfamiliar with the archives, we were trying to keep this project as low impact as possible. In addition, we wanted to be sure that our own student employees, who have no formal professional training, would be able to use and understand the new tool. Our students gave us valuable feedback, and we made adjustments to the information displays based on their suggestions.

Feeling confident that the document blog posts themselves were relatively intuitive, we turned to other considerations, such as how descriptive fields should be provided as limiting options on the search screen, which ones should be available for browsing, and how search and browse results should display. Because the software is so flexible, it seemed at times that there was an almost endless stream of questions and possibilities to address. Thankfully, the system is so easily manipulated that we could approach these issues in an iterative fashion, making small changes as we went along. If we weren't happy with the result, we could change things back or simply try something else. Once we were satisfied with the look and functionality of the blog, we returned to our Academic Technology contact one last time to finalize the changes that required more advanced programming skills. Altogether, this final configuration and testing phase of the implementation process lasted about two weeks.

Done with our testing, we needed to decide how best to approach the selection of material for the blog. One method would be to simply have the items described in call number order, working methodically through the black file cabinets from the first folder to the last. The subjects of our most frequent requests, however, are known to us because of data collected through our reference blog. To ensure that more popular and desirable items were made available first, we decided to start with materials related to the most high-profile and sought-after people associated with the college, such as Benjamin Rush, James Buchanan, Spencer Fullerton Baird, and Joseph Priestley. We searched through the black file cabinets to identify such items and targeted those for upload first.

With the design process completed, items prioritized for entry, and several test posts serving as samples, we asked one of our more experienced senior work/study employees to begin composing additional posts for the document blog. We provided training on the blogging process and instruction on how to draft appropriate descriptions. Based on usage information from our reference blog and our earlier web projects, we knew that proper nouns were typically the primary element in people's keyword searches that led them to our sites. Beyond the use of people's names in the title of the blog entry and in the People tag field, we stressed to our student the importance of including relevant proper nouns in the narrative free-text descriptions. We encouraged the student to take as much time as was needed to examine and interrogate the document, to ask us questions if anything was unclear, and to describe the key issues, individuals, places, or events that were represented (see figure 11.2).

After the student had crafted about 20 document posts, we evaluated them for accuracy, consistency, and completeness. As expected, we found minor typographical errors, but aside from that we found the posts to be good, if sometimes brief, representations of the items themselves. Based on her experience, the student also made some observations and suggestions regarding the workflow. For the remainder of the semester, we continued tinkering with issues regarding priorities for selection of items to be described and quality control of posts. The student continued to

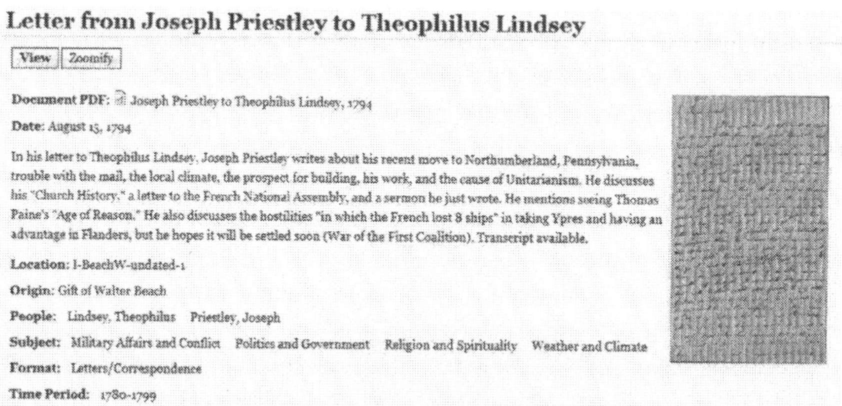
Letter from Joseph Priestley to Theophilus Lindsey

View | Zoomify

Document PDF: Joseph Priestley to Theophilus Lindsey, 1794

Date: August 15, 1794

In his letter to Theophilus Lindsey, Joseph Priestley writes about his recent move to Northumberland, Pennsylvania, trouble with the mail, the local climate, the prospect for building, his work, and the cause of Unitarianism. He discusses his "Church History," a letter to the French National Assembly, and a sermon he just wrote. He mentions seeing Thomas Paine's "Age of Reason." He also discusses the hostilities "in which the French lost 8 ships" in taking Ypres and having an advantage in Flanders, but he hopes it will be settled soon (War of the First Coalition). Transcript available.

Location: I-BeachW-undated-1

Origin: Gift of Walter Beach

People: Lindsey, Theophilus Priestley, Joseph

Subject: Military Affairs and Conflict Politics and Government Religion and Spirituality Weather and Climate

Format: Letters/Correspondence

Time Period: 1780–1799

Figure 11.2. Example of a document blog post.

craft entries for the document blog throughout the next three months, completing about 200 entries by the time she graduated in May 2011.

During the following academic year, we were fortunate to have the services of a full-time paid intern. This intern, as part of her many duties, continued to create new blog posts. By March of 2012, we added two more short-term members to our team—one a paid intern aspiring to graduate work in archives and the other a newly minted library professional with a strong computer background. With this additional, if temporary, workforce, we decided to pursue other major changes to the Archives and Special Collections website. We wanted not only to build on the success of the Drupal-based model of the document and reference blogs but also to migrate historical information from other HTML-based sites created over the past 12 years.

The new website that we were able to develop with the help of this team significantly improved our search functionalities by creating a separate blog for complete manuscript collections, a partner to the document blog that now shared the same tag fields. Those shared fields meant that the new collections blog could now be cross-searched and sorted with the document blog. For the first time, we had a single website where all of our primary information could be discovered, browsed, and searched, as shown in figure 11.1.

RESULTS

By all of our measures, the document blog has thus far proven to be a success.[5] More than 700 items from the black file cabinets have been described, scanned, and uploaded to the website by students and interns over the past two and a half years. These items, previously invisible to the world and thus completely underutilized, now have a global audience. In addition, we have scanned and uploaded numerous other items drawn from our various manuscript collections in response to researcher requests. Items such as these were previously discoverable only through their finding aids, but the document blog now offers another means for discovery, in addition to providing easy access to the content and making more efficient use of staff time.

Visitors to the document blog over the past year have numbered a little over 2,000, and the traffic reflects a steady upward trend in the number of visitors to our site. During the most recently completed quarter, the blog averaged 186 users per month—a far cry from the handful of patrons from outside the college community who typically would visit the reading room for their own research needs. Google search engines, unsurprisingly, bring in roughly 52 percent of all visitors to the blog, with all other search engines accounting for less than 4 percent of our traffic and social media sites bringing in just under 2 percent.

Just a little over a year since the launch of our new archives website in the summer of 2012, we have also begun to see cases of outside websites linking directly to individual items in our document blog, driving further traffic to our site and making the discovery and access process more efficient for patrons interested in our unique holdings. The Three Mile Island report by Hyman Rickover, mentioned earlier, is one notable example of such external linking, being included in a blog post on nuclear safety and management site as well as a science open-access search site. It is because of these kinds of connections that the Rickover report is currently the most visited individual post on the document blog, accounting for nearly 6 percent of all traffic to the site over the past year.

One great benefit of this project for the permanent staff is that we are becoming more aware of these black file cabinet items through the document blog processes. Reviewing and selecting items for the students to describe provides a kind of introduction to what is available in these often overlooked files. Following up with a review of the blog posts crafted by the students then provides the staff with more information about the document, revealing things we might not have been familiar with at all or perhaps just needed to be reminded of. It is this personal knowledge that can be so helpful when providing reference services to researchers or when discussing with faculty members the materials that may be relevant to a particular course they are teaching.

Besides the value of this project for permanent staff, the undergraduate students and interns who examine and describe materials for the document blog have reported enjoying this activity, finding it both interesting and, at times, challenging. The work itself exposes our students to different types of information, formats, and processes that are often unfamiliar. Depending on the document, they may struggle with deciphering handwriting, with discerning the meaning and intent of the document and its creator, or with crafting a reasonable descriptive summary of the document. In the end, though, they have all responded positively to the intellectual rigor of the activity. Strong evidence of their satisfaction is the degree to which they share with their fellow undergraduate employees interesting things that they learn from the documents they describe. The win–win–win is that our undergraduate workers can earn a salary, increase their own personal knowledge and expertise, and contribute to a learning environment that benefits users around the globe. For us, positive outcomes for our student workers are an important element of the success of the project.[6]

LESSONS LEARNED

Our initial plan called for scanning in two phases, with Phase 1 facilitating discovery and Phase 2 facilitating access. For items in the black file cabinets, we planned to scan and upload only the first page of the document, in the interest of time, at the moment a student or intern crafted a blog post. Our assumption was that time would be saved by fully scanning only those documents specifically requested by researchers, which would likely be just a percentage of the total holdings. This approach meant that even items of potentially high interest but not yet specifically requested would need to be handled twice—once for the initial scan and post, and then a second time when and if a complete copy of the document was requested.

One drawback to this approach that we had not initially anticipated was the confusion that this would cause for our online patrons. With the descriptive information and an image of the first page of any given document, many users assumed that no additional pages were extant. (This confusion was heightened by our oversight in not including the number of pages of the item in our metadata schema or in our narrative descriptions.) Rather than asking for more complete information, many users just figured that everything available was already online and that the item itself was only one page long. Thus, this approach, while saving time during input, was not effective for conveying the extent of the information available. As a result, we have altered our approach so that the complete item is scanned and shared online from the beginning, with no need for a second phase. Discovery and access are now supported simultaneously.

In terms of workflow, one of the greatest challenges is finding time for basic quality control activities. There are always going to be minor errors with any individual blog post, whether created by a student or professional. While student and intern schedules are relatively regular, permanent staff members are subject to many unplanned demands upon their time. That often means that blog posts are not reviewed as soon after they are posted as we might like. In the interest of making information available as quickly as possible, we decided early on not to have the unreviewed blog posts wait in a "draft" state for our approval. We felt this approach was inconsistent with the goal of making materials "discoverable" as quickly as possible. As a compromise solution, we have added student reviewing to our workflow, with undergraduate peer editing providing a way to catch and fix basic typographical errors in a timely fashion.

Similarly, the ease with which a document blog post can be corrected and updated allows us a certain freedom from worrying that each description should be "perfect" at the time the entry is first posted. Students and interns viewing a single item for the first time are not likely to have much personal knowledge of the subject matter or the individuals involved, or to have context for the creation of the document itself. We therefore accept that descriptions can, and likely will, be edited and expanded over time. In much the same way that we update finding aids when new information comes to light, so too will we update posts on the document blog as necessary and desirable.

Because of the difficulty inherent in making sense of a single document out of context, as much as possible we try to have our students and interns create blog posts and edit existing blog entries that are within their own personal areas of interest or expertise. If a person has more knowledge of a particular subject or time period or culture represented in an item, then that person will likely understand the context and significance of the item more readily and will also be more likely to describe the item in greater detail and with more accuracy.

Besides subject knowledge, an important consideration when assigning individuals to work on the document blog is the personality of the student or intern. We are well aware that this kind of work is not for everyone. Students who are more inquisitive and exploratory are likely to craft better descriptions. They will interrogate the documents more thoroughly, talk with their fellow students, and ask questions of archives staff and even faculty members. The students who talk about the items they've blogged, enthusiastically sharing what they've learned with their fellow undergraduates, are clearly engaged and interested. Those who remain quiet throughout the process, ask few questions, and simply "go through the motions" are students who need a different work assignment.

In addition to workflow and personnel issues, one significant lesson learned regards the black file cabinet documents themselves. For the most part, these items reflect acquisitions from the 1950s through the present day. Prior to this project, the permanent staff members had relatively little familiarity with the full contents of the black file cabinets. Through the process of selecting items for scanning and uploading during the early testing and development of the document blog, we learned quite a bit about the materials related to some of the more popularly researched individuals and topics.

However, as we continued to review the contents of the black file cabinets, we discovered a lot of material that seemed to warrant reappraisal. Many of the items purchased by librarians in the mid-20th century reflected the approach of autograph collecting, with material being acquired for the name association of a famous individual rather than for the usefulness of the content for teaching and learning purposes at the college. Rather than indiscriminately adding every item in the black file cabinets to the document blog, we have chosen instead to reevaluate them all first. We are currently examining the contents of each file to assess its appropriateness for our collections, and we plan to deaccession those items that do not fit our collection development criteria. In the end, the document blog project will have helped us to sharpen this collection of single-item purchases and donations in addition to making the materials themselves more easily discoverable and accessible.

In this regard, our strategy of prioritizing adding materials to the blog by starting first with items related to our list of notables was a wise one. All of those materials are ones that we will certainly be keeping. We are now reviewing the remainder of the 3,000 folders, working through them in call number order. Once we determine that the materials are still relevant to our collecting policy and our institution's needs, we then put them in the queue for the students to upload and describe.

CONCLUSION

For us, the document blog has provided the best solution, within the constraints of our available human and technical resources, to the problem of exposing an underutilized collection of single-item purchases and donations. The blog has also provided an environment to share other materials digitized on demand, making all of these items both discoverable and accessible.

The success of the document blog has provided inspiration for us, and we have begun to create subject-based catablogs, an information resource similar to online library guides. Given the ease with which new blogs may be developed within our Drupal instance, we see such subject catablogs as a simple way to showcase materials around a particular event or topic. In light of the 150th anniversary of the Confederate invasion of the town of Carlisle in the summer of 1863, we decided to experiment with this model by developing a Civil War resources blog. Within weeks of designing the blog and uploading a few dozen posts, we received a message from a well-published historian who had discovered the site in the course of his research. In writing to request further information, he commented that our Civil War blog was "one the best archives sites" he'd seen.

This subject-based catablog approach offers us a new way to expose largely hidden and underutilized resources within our collections. Much like an exhibit, such a blog allows us to bring together on one site materials that are widely scattered among our holdings. Even further, we are able to develop unique tag fields for each subject, which will in turn allow a more useful and specific searching and sorting experience for interested patrons. Finally, we can invite our students and interns to populate subject catablogs that align with their own personal knowledge and interests. A student with extensive military history research experience made valuable contributions to our Civil War catablog this past summer, while an intern with knowledge of Russian language and culture is currently gathering materials for new a catablog on that topic.

Besides developing subject-specific search tools, we are also beginning to address an issue related to the longer-term viability of the information stored in our document blog and the other Drupal-based resources we have developed. While we know that we can easily export our metadata if and when needed, we would like the metadata to be compliant with a standard that other systems may utilize. For the document blog specifically, we are considering further changes to our metadata schema that will align with DACS. We will then develop a plan for implementation of these changes in the near future.

In an age where scarcity of resources leaves most description being done at only the collection or series level, the attention we are paying to individual items might not seem like the best approach. From our perspective, though, these blogging efforts succeed on multiple fronts. Previously hidden and underused materials not only become discoverable but also easily accessible to a worldwide audience, and evidence shows that these documents are being well used. In addition, the activity of developing the document blog makes our permanent staff members more aware of these relatively neglected resources and better able to provide effective reference service to patrons interested in topics that may be informed by these materials.

Perhaps most importantly, though, students and interns enjoy a valuable and worthwhile learning experience that, in many cases, aligns well with their own interests and furthers their own educational, and even career goals. Undergraduate student employees and interns have made valuable contributions to the Archives and Special Collections Department at Dickinson College for nearly 40 years. The number of researchers who have benefited from their efforts serves as a testament to their efforts, and the number of former student employees who go on to careers in the information professions is a testament to their own dedication to their work. With the document blog, and now with new subject catablogs, our students and interns are continuing that tradition.

James Gerencser *is the college archivist at Dickinson College.*

NOTES

1. Website at http://archives.dickinson.edu/research_requests_blog. For more information about this reference blog, see Malinda Triller, "Double-Duty Blogging: A Reference Blog for Management and Outreach," in *A Different Kind of Web: New Connections between Archives and Our Users*, ed. Kate Theimer (Chicago: Society of American Archivists, 2011), 203–12.

2. Although the roughly 3,000 items continue to be referred to using the term "black file cabinets," in actuality the documents themselves were refoldered and rehoused in archival boxes during the summer of 2000 in response to storage and preservation concerns. Though more than 10 years have passed, no other name besides "black file cabinets" has yet emerged for this aggregation of single-item accessions.

3. For more information about the concept of the catablog, see Robert S. Cox and Danielle Kovacs, "Alice in the Archives: The Evolution of the Catablog," in *A Different Kind of Web: New Connections between Archives and Our Users*, ed. Kate Theimer (Chicago: Society of American Archivists, 2011), 180–90.

4. Website at http://coeducation.dickinson.edu. For a description of the project, see Malinda Triller, "Social Networking Software in the Archives: Using Blogs to Engage Students with Primary Sources," in *Past or Portal? Enhancing Undergraduate Learning through Special Collections and Archives*, ed. Eleanor Mitchell, Peggy Seiden, and Suzy Taraba (Chicago: Association of College and Research Libraries, 2012), 255–60.

5. The website for the Archives and Special Collections can be found at http://archives.dickinson.edu/, and the document blog can be found at http://archives.dickinson.edu/collections_documents/browse_document_descriptions.

6. For information about a survey of our work/study undergraduates and assessment of outcomes, see James Gerencser, "Finding Value and Meaning through Work/Study in the Archives," in *Past or Portal? Enhancing Undergraduate Learning through Special Collections and Archives*, ed. Eleanor Mitchell, Peggy Seiden, and Suzy Taraba (Chicago: Association of College and Research Libraries, 2012), 248–54.

Index

About the Editor

Kate Theimer is the author of the popular blog *ArchivesNext* and a frequent writer, speaker, and commentator on issues related to the future of archives. She is the author of *Web 2.0 Tools and Strategies for Archives and Local History Collections* and the editor of *A Different Kind of Web: New Connections between Archives and Our Users*, as well having contributed chapters to *Many Happy Returns: Advocacy for Archives and Archivists*, *The Future of Archives and Recordkeeping*, and the forthcoming *Encyclopedia of Archival Concepts, Principles, and Practices*. She has published articles in *The American Archivist* and the *Journal of Digital Humanities*.

Kate served on the Council of the Society of American Archivists from 2010 to 2013. Before starting her career as an independent writer and editor, she worked in the policy division of the National Archives and Records Administration in College Park, Maryland. She holds an MSI with a specialization in archives and records management from the University of Michigan and an MA in art history from the University of Maryland.

53612362R00124

Made in the USA
San Bernardino, CA
22 September 2017